VICTORY

ALSO BY LARRY BROUGHTON

FLASHPOINTS for achievers:
Inspiring messages that bring significant results, a daily journal

REVEALED! 8 Mission Tested Strategies for Success in Life &
Leadership

VICTORY: 7 Entrepreneurial Success Strategies for Veterans
(Co-Author)

Boots to Business: Introduction to Business Ownership
For Veterans and Military Service Members
(Co-Author)

To learn more about Larry, please visit
www.LarryBroughton.me

VICTORY

7 REVOLUTIONARY STRATEGIES FOR ENTREPRENEURS TO LAUNCH YOUR BUSINESS, ELEVATE YOUR IMPACT AND TRANSFORM YOUR LIFE

go get 'em!

Larry Broughton

D. O. L.

LARRY BROUGHTON

BANDERA
—PUBLISHING—

Published by Bandera Publishing, 2400 E. Katella Ave, Suite 800, Anaheim, CA 92806

Broughton, Larry
    VICTORY: 7 Revolutionary Strategies for Entrepreneurs to Launch Your Business, Elevate Your Impact and Transform Your Life
    Paperback ISBN: 978-0-9982848-2-8

First edition published in 2011 by Bandera Publishing

Cover design: Joe Potter
Back cover photo: Westover Photography
Interior design: Deanne Marie

IN PRAISE OF VICTORY

It's not attraction, it's ACTION that powers your success. This book is a blueprint on how to achieve VICTORY on the business battlefield by tapping into your unconquerable warrior spirit.

— Darren Hardy
New York Times bestselling author, former publisher of SUCCESS Magazine
DarrenHardy.com

This powerful, action-oriented book is based on years of sustained entrepreneurial victories, by a guy who has been there and done that. Using Broughton's business battle plan detailed in VICTORY, every entrepreneur can tap into their warrior spirit, and face the business battlefield with courage. Be warned: VICTORY is contagious.

— Brian Tracy
Speaker and author of *The Way to Wealth* and *Maximum Achievement*
BrianTracy.com

Larry presents a simple, yet provocative approach to entrepreneurial success: Action Is Power! Any business can find success if VICTORY is the only option.

— Tony Hsieh
Author of #1 *New York Times* bestseller, *Delivering Happiness*
CEO, Zappos
Zappos.com

VICTORY brilliantly shows how the same warrior ethos that serves our military members in battle, serves our entrepreneur class in the business arena. It's often the simplest of ideas that are the most profound: take rapid, decisive action; make course corrections along the way; never surrender; and serve others. With VICTORY Broughton becomes the vanguard of the Entrepreneur Revolution.

— Chip Conley
Founder and Executive Chair, Joie de Vivre Hospitality
Author, *PEAK: How Great Companies Get Their Mojo from Maslow*
ChipConley.com

Teammates, it is an honor to introduce you to VICTORY, Larry Broughton's tested and true action plan of a book. Larry's a remarkable entrepreneur and a man on a mission to help others defy the odds. I hope you find him as inspiring as I do. I believe you'll find his message one that will help you to NEVER GIVE UP ON YOUR DREAMS! Would-be entrepreneurs, VICTORY is a book that will help you unlock your dreams and make them a reality. Lock 'n Load!

— Alden Mills
Former Navy SEAL
Author of *Be Unstoppable: 8 Essential Actions to Succeed at Anything*
Alden-Mills.com

As a former fighter pilot turned entrepreneur, I found VICTORY to be a hard-hitting, fast-paced, and to-the-point presentation on achieving success. Let's face it ... Larry has been there, done that ... and he's still doing it today. In my mind, he is one of the nation's leading "Top Guns" for showing people like us how to get more done in less time, make more money, and take more time off. Get the book, read it ... and then read it again. It's just that good.

— Ed Rush
Speaker and Author of Fighter Pilot Performance for Business
EdRush.com

VICTORY has been in my business tool box since the day I started this entrepreneurial journey! Learning to work with your strengths and delegating the rest has been vital to my personal and business growth, as well as developing systems to get things done. This book will give you a map to go forth and conquer while giving you guidance on making a lasting impact with your entrepreneurial endeavors. Pick this book up and find a pen and paper because you will need to participate in the process of creating your future!

— Tammi Moses
Chief Encouragement Officer, Homes are for Living
HomesAreForLiving.com

Every entrepreneur knows it, every warrior lives it, and VICTORY reinforces it: inaction is worse than failure! This book captures the wisdom gained by sustained entrepreneurial victory, and the agony of business defeat. Do not venture on to the business battlefield alone ... use VICTORY as your guide!

— Jonathan Sprinkles
TV analyst, Featured columnist, Former National Speaker of the Year
JSprinkles.com

In VICTORY, Larry gives straightforward, no-nonsense strategies that helped me see myself as a business owner in a new way. By applying the strategies I learned in the book, our company not only survived, but thrived through one of the worst industry downturns in history. Now, I'm expanding what's possible not just for my company, but for my life as well.

— Bobbie Hurley
Co-Owner / Vice President, Arpco Valves & Controls
BobbieHurley.com

In my line of work, I have the great fortune of getting to know countless entrepreneurs. Larry is one of the few that I would describe as an exemplar for anyone who aspires to business ownership. VICTORY is a great place to start learning from this master. This book, with its inspired and practical strategies, is a must for anyone who thinks business ownership might be in their future. Even seasoned entrepreneurs will benefit from these battle-tested principles from a veteran business innovator.

— Dr. Mike Haynie, PhD
Vice Chancellor, Syracuse University
Barnes Professor of Entrepreneurship

CONTENTS

ACKNOWLEDGEMENTS

The first edition of this book had been swirling around in my imagination for several years prior to its first publication, but it wasn't until the sparks began to fly during a brainstorming session with my co-author of that first edition in 2010 that it all came together. There's no better feeling in the business world than collaborating on a project with like-minded teammates who are simpatico, who share a heart for serving others, the drive to make a difference, and the determination to get things done. That's how things were during the initial process and release of VICTORY, and that feeling and energy was even more apparent during the creation of the new material, content, sketches, and tools I developed with my team for the upgraded and expanded 2nd Edition of this powerful book.

The ideas, concepts and writing are based on years of trial and error in the leadership and entrepreneurial arena. The completion of this book project, however, would not have been possible without the help and support of dozens of people around me who believe in me, and the value of this book's message. Frankly, I've been in awe at the number of late hours the editors, graphic artists, and formatting team have been willing to work on this project to get it out of my head and hard drive, and into bookstores. I continue to be surprised and humbled by the growing support among fellow entrepreneurs who have committed to join the vanguard of what I've been calling the Entrepreneur Revolution.

Personal Thanks from Larry Broughton:

My deepest gratitude goes out to the following: **my friends and teammates** for believing in me, and encouraging me during the ups and downs of the entrepreneurial journey; my kids, **Emily** and **Ben**, who see me at my goofiest and still think I'm the bee's knees; **Suzanne Moshenko**, the amazing mother of my kids, whose flexibility with my crazy travel schedule is invaluable as I crisscross the country leading our efforts at broughtonHOTELS, supporting and cheering on coaching clients, making television appearances, and honing my messages as I deliver keynote speech presentations to entrepreneurs, conferences, fundraisers, corporate boardrooms and anyone else who will heed my call; marketing genius **Donny Deutsch** who first encouraged me to get my thoughts into book form while on the set of his entrepreneurial show on CNBC; executive mentor and former Publisher of SUCCESS magazine **Darren Hardy**, who reminded me of the power of encouraging and succinct emails by simply saying, "Bravo! Damn, always GREAT stuff," referring to my FLASHPOINTS email messages (which later became a transformational book that's reached tens of thousands of readers) … his timing was perfect.

Special thanks also to the host of MSNBC's *Your Business,* **JJ Ramberg,** who graciously agreed to write the Foreword to this book and somehow keeps allowing me to come back on her successful long-running show for small business owners; **my SF brothers** at 10th and 12th Special Forces Groups, particularly the guys at ODA 064 and ODA 1275 who taught me the power of love, tenacity, and honor; all our **military service members and veterans** who have dared to pick up the sword and shield to serve causes greater than themselves that allows me the freedom to pursue my own capitalist goals; my friend and hotelier twin, host of Travel Channel's hit show *Hotel Impossible*, **Anthony Melchiorri**, who offers continual encouragement, support and laughs, and generously offered to write the Afterword for this book; my executive assistant and office manager **Melissa Papke** who rallied and prioritized the hundreds of other projects I have in the works, and spent countless hours with the publisher, editors and designers, proofing and offering that valuable extra set of eyes we all need in our pursuits; my older brother **Bryan Broughton**, who in his dying showed me that life is too short not to follow your dreams; my twin brother **Barry Broughton** for being one of my heroes, one of the toughest SOBs to walk the planet, and for showing me that we must follow our passions, even if it means changing directions.

A heartfelt thanks: to the powerhouse **Executive Team** of stallions at **broughtonHOTELS** who seem to tolerate me and keep the organization growing when I'm distracted with my many entrepreneurial adventures, I would be in an asylum if not for each of them; to my business and executive coaching partner at all things yoogozi.com, my friend who stood by me during some of my darkest hours, **Dave Braun,** who is the yin to my entrepreneurial yang; and **Melodee Meyers** and **Bridget Brady** for encouraging me, trusting me, and even sharing tips, stories and pitfalls of their book publishing adventures.

My sincerest appreciation: to all my current and past **Mastermind members and coaching clients**, for allowing me to be their guide, and letting me learn so much about myself during the process, and for sharing their stories and lessons, many of which shape this book; to **Nell Daly** for inspiring me with her courage and willingness to walk into the lion's den time and again offering a voice for the weak, misunderstood, and forgotten … the world needs more voices like hers; to my friend, writing partner, and organizer of my spaghetti pot of ideas and thoughts, **Deanne Marie**, without whom this 2nd Edition would still be locked away in my mind, I am humbled by her many talents; and **God** for giving me another chance (again and again) for His grace, and speaking words of love and encouragement through my inner voice.

Special thanks to all those folks who told me I'd be risking the security of a well-respected job and healthy paycheck if I started my own companies, and then "encouraged" me *not* to venture on the entrepreneurial journey, to turn back and stay in the calm waters, and told me it was scary out there past the horizon. You know what? They were right, and I wouldn't have it any other way!

FOREWORD

By JJ Ramberg
Host, Your Business *on MSNBC*

I met Larry at a women's entrepreneur event where we were each delivering a keynote address. I was struck by his no-nonsense approach and his heartfelt desire to serve others on the entrepreneurial path. I immediately invited him to be a guest on my show. Since then, we have developed a friendship and mutual admiration, and he's come back on *Your Business* many times offering up great insight to our viewers.

This book is written from that practical, straightforward business perspective. In these pages you'll find Larry's 30 years of entrepreneurial experience broken down into easy to follow and implement modules. I say they're easy to follow, but what I've seen with countless small business owners—myself included—is that building your business takes consistent action and, well, hard work.

Twelve years ago, I started my own company, Goodshop. Before that, I had been a financial reporter and gotten my MBA. But while I had studied so much about business, there are just some things you have to learn by doing—in the trenches. In this book, Larry takes those things and teaches you how to avoid common pitfalls (like the Lone Wolf Syndrome) and lay an essential foundation for your business.

For example, don't underestimate the importance of creating and communicating a strong, clear vision for your business (the "V" in VICTORY). When I was reporting for CNN in Biloxi, MS and New Orleans in the aftermath of Hurricane Katrina, I knew I had to do something for the people in these cities, and for all the causes around the country. My brother and I had this big, crazy idea of creating a place where people can do what they normally would do online—search the internet and shop online—and have money donated to a cause of their choice. It was turning that idea into a vision that suddenly galvanized a team and a movement around us to make our site a reality. I'm proud to say that our users and shoppers have raised nearly $13 million for causes around the world.

Whether you're just starting out and launching your business, or you're somewhat established and now you want to expand your reach and impact, or you've realized that your business has swallowed your life and you need more balance, you'll find valuable, take-action advice in this book.

Being an entrepreneur is one of the most rewarding journeys anyone can take. There will be endless days and sleepless nights, times when you feel on top of the world, and times when you'll question if any of it is worth it. It is, I assure you. Apply the strategies and principles laid out in this book and you'll be well on your way to making your business dreams a reality, impacting the lives of people you may never meet in ways you never dreamed of, and leaving a legacy far beyond your imagination.

Welcome to the Entrepreneur Revolution!

JJ Ramberg
Host of *Your Business* on MSNBC
Author of *It's Your Business: 183 Essential Tips that Will Transform Your Small Business*
Co-founder of Goodshop.com

 @msnbcYourBiz

 @msnbcYourBusiness

READ THIS FIRST!

L ock 'n load! We're moving out!" Even if you've never served in the military, that phrase grabs your attention and gets your adrenaline pumping. It's brief, it's descriptive ... and when you hear it, you know it's time for quick action.

I'm committed to encouraging this same mindset in addressing the issues faced by current and aspiring entrepreneurs—because frankly, I'm pissed off by what I see! Day in and day out I see potential-filled people led down the wrong path, wasting their valuable time and precious money, getting frustrated as they struggle to launch their dream of entrepreneurship, only to see it fade away into yesterday.

Here's what you can expect from this Second Edition of VICTORY: straight talk; zero BS; expanded and more pertinent chapter content; sketches, graphs, and graphics to help distill and encapsulate concepts; and an action-oriented approach to help propel you and your business towards a life of significance— *and* success.

Before I go any further, let me make a bold statement: If you want a life of self-determination, high reward, high social impact, prestige, economic freedom, and legacy, STOP CHASING SUCCESS!

Seeking success for success's sake will leave you hollow, emotionally depleted, spiritually void, devastatingly depressed, and ultimately forgotten. Rather, I plead with you to seek a life of *significance*, not success. Play a *significant* role in the lives of those in your community, family, business, and place of worship (if that's your bag) by serving to help *them* reach *their* fullest potential. The universe has a crazy way of rewarding those who serve others before serving themselves.

When we serve others, we become attractive to other high achievers who want to rally around us to help us reach our goals and fullest potential. There's no time or room on the entrepreneurial journey for the Lone Wolf strategy. That Lone Wolf myth makes for great movies and romance novels, but it's a load of crap when it comes to the reality of entrepreneurship and living of a life of significance. The path of entrepreneurship can be a lonely one that can lead to a cliff of oblivion unless we intentionally engage in building a community of supportive teammates. Surround yourself with like-minded high-achievers and get ready to soar!

The late, great personal development guru Jim Rohn famously said, "you become the average of the five people you hang out with the most." Sure, that's some sage advice, but it means we need to make some tough choices. Are you surrounded by fear mongers, chickens, and turkeys; or are you soaring with eagles?

Who Are You Giving Your Time To?

Darren Hardy, the former Publisher of SUCCESS Magazine described for me over dinner one night several years ago at the beautiful Lodge at Torrey Pines in La Jolla, California, that there are 5-Minute people, 5-Month people and 5-Year people in our lives. He encouraged me not to confuse them.

He said 5-Minute people might be one of those neighbors we have brief conversations with over the fence about the weather, but when it goes longer than five minutes, their negativity brings us down, we feel disgusted or dirty and want to go take a shower. 5-Month people are those we enjoy and can learn from, can do short projects with, and even share a coffee, drink, or meal. 5-Year people are those with whom we make lasting commitments, do life's journey with, and invite into our homes for holiday meals and celebrations.

Just because we have negative or toxic 5-Minute people as neighbors or family members, doesn't mean we are required to take advice from them, engage with them, or invite them to Christmas dinner.

If you take nothing else from this book, I hope you grasp the concept that many of the world's most loved, influential, brilliant, and enduring entrepreneurs, leaders, and high achievers have shared in various forms: *there is no higher calling than serving others.*

The simple, yet powerful, truth is that *success is the byproduct of significance.*

You've very likely picked up this book because you are one of a very special group of people. You're among the high achievers, the risk-takers, the visionaries, and the trail blazers; those who have decided to start their *own* business ... and we are most definitely a dedicated and tenacious bunch.

So as of now, you may be thinking, "So what? What does that have to do with *me* and *my* business?" Great question! The short answer is that I have extensively studied, evaluated, and synthesized the attitudes, mindset, business tactics, and entrepreneurial strategies that support this repeatable success. Rest assured, what you learn in this book will absolutely work for you and your business—if you take rapid action, and consistently apply the small, simple, powerful tools presented herein!

Stepping Into The Gap

America is suffering from an ever-widening leadership gap in every segment of society: political, religious, business, and academia. Entrepreneurs are uniquely qualified to close this leadership gap because we're always looking for ways to be better, do better, respond faster, and produce more.

A poll I read a couple of years ago said that 63 percent of Americans think our best years as a nation are behind us. Frankly, I think they're wrong. But how do we, as leaders, change that? By stepping into the leadership gap. By telling our stories and sharing our vision of how things can be.

As entrepreneurs in America, I firmly believe that we still have the goods. We still have the greatest ideas. We've got passion in our hearts and fire in our guts. And yes, there are obstacles. Sometimes those obstacles are educational, sometimes financial, sometimes governmental. But when we take action, we can overcome those obstacles, and that's where this book will help you navigate some of the rough waters in starting and running your own business.

ANATOMY OF THE ENTREPRENEUR

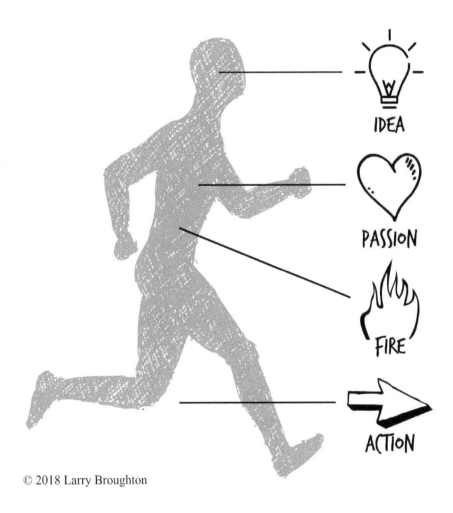

Sure, our government tries its best to help out entrepreneurs. Fortunately, I've had the opportunity to audit many of the programs available through the Small Business Administration and various other resources that are ostensibly designed to support you and your entrepreneurial spirit. Unfortunately, after reviewing those audits and laying it out on the line, I can say that I'm unimpressed.

While some innovative initiatives do exist, many of these well-intentioned programs are only marginally successful in helping entrepreneurs to open, manage, and grow their businesses.

So why aren't these programs more successful? Most of the people who coordinate and administer them ARE genuinely trying to help. Unfortunately, many of those who formulate, teach and implement key decisions within these programs are bureaucrats or former employees and executives who worked for some other business, and have never actually started or ran their own successful business! They do not have the hands-on knowledge of the unique challenges that come with entrepreneurship.

In addition to this, the lack of practical experience in marketing, team building, and the growth strategies critical for achieving sustainable success in today's changing business world is a recipe for disaster. Ultimately, very few of them share the unique combination of the discipline, drive and "make it happen" attitude that literally *defines* many of society's greatest entrepreneurs.

I strongly believe that you, the modern-day entrepreneur, need more tools in your toolkit than archaic formulas, generic advice, and one-size-fits-all "solutions." You need a customizable plan of action, one based on specific success strategies that apply to a business of any size, whether it's a one-person operation, a small ensemble firm, or a national (maybe even international) multi-site company being structured for public or private sale.

In this book, you'll discover the proven success strategies you need to effectively build and grow your business. These strategies represent a premium distillation of what I've used in my 30+ years of entrepreneurial and leadership experience; along with the top tips I've gleaned from interviewing, mentoring, and coaching literally hundreds of high-achieving entrepreneurs and CEOs over the past ten years.

The strategies I'll talk about, when consistently applied, will enable you to achieve financial success with your business and empower you to build the organization that directly reflects your own individual passion, brilliance, skills, and core values. You will also discover how to connect with your ideal clients and use your ideas to help support your family, your community, and the broader world.

Keep in mind that these are not simply my *theories* concerning what *might* work in business. These theories are mission-tested, practical, and *actionable* ideas anyone can use to improve their business. Maybe you've got a powerful business idea and the passion to make it a reality; maybe you're an entrepreneur who has already been in business a couple of years but are drowning in the sea of conflicting priorities that arise as your business grows. Maybe you're even a highly successful entrepreneur who's hoping to find a few tips or "secret weapons" you can use to elevate your business to the next level, or you want to get a jump on the competition.

Whatever your unique case may be, you will find something in this book to help you.

At this point, you might be asking yourself, "Why should I believe this guy? How does he know what makes for a successful entrepreneur?" Those are valid questions and I promised you straight answers - so here's the deal:

Who Am I?

That's a great question. I'm Larry Broughton. I've celebrated the thrill of business victories and have suffered the agony of business defeats. I understand the tremendous value of actually making mistakes in business, learning from those mistakes, making course corrections along the way, and then NOT repeating those same mistakes. There's absolutely no substitute for applied, real-life experience!

Most importantly, I've been exactly where *you* are right now, whether you're facing the excitement and fear of starting your first business, you're already up and running but faced with daunting obstacles to growth, or you're ready to "go national" and beyond. Please allow me to share a little more of my background and how you can best use this book ... then we'll dive right in!

My Story

I spent nearly eight years on Special Forces A-Teams (commonly known as the Green Berets) in the U.S. Army, where I traveled the world and attained the rank of Staff Sergeant. I then took the lessons I learned there and applied them to the business arena. As a serial entrepreneur, I've built, bought, and sold several businesses, and I'm the founder and CEO of broughtonHOTELS, a nationally known, multi-unit, award-winning hospitality company considered a leader in the boutique hotel industry.

I've been honored to receive several business awards, including Ernst & Young's *Entrepreneur of the Year Award®*. The National Veteran-Owned Business Association named me their *Vetrepreneur® of the Year*; Coastline Foundation named me their *Visionary of the Year*; Passkeys Foundation honored me with their prestigious *National Business Leader of Integrity* award; and Entrepreneur Magazine included broughtonHOTELS on their "*Hot 500 List of Fastest Growing Privately Held Companies.*"

I've interviewed nearly 200 successful business owners, entrepreneurs, and high-achievers asking them the hard questions about what they did right, what they did wrong, and how they would do it better the next time around. I've also directly coached and mentored hundreds of leaders and entrepreneurs, helping them launch and grow their businesses by connecting the dots and applying the lessons learned by those trail blazers who have gone before them. (You'll hear several of these real-life VICTORY success stories from business owners I've mentored throughout the book.)

I've also authored several articles and books on leadership, elite team building, and entrepreneurial significance (in addition to traveling internationally to deliver keynote presentations on these topics) and have been featured in newspaper and magazine articles across the country. I've enjoyed the privilege of being invited to appear as a guest expert on national radio, news, and TV programs on every major network in the country. I'm happy to be living an absolutely blessed life!

The principles in this book are those I've personally used to create, operate, and grow several successful businesses. They're peer-reviewed and confirmed effective by colleagues and successful entrepreneurs across the country. I'm convinced they can help you do the same!

How This Book Is Organized

I've crafted this book with three primary goals in mind:

★ To give you concise information with a minimal amount of fluff;

★ To provide relevant examples of the principles in the book from the lives of fellow entrepreneurs who have achieved high levels of success using these strategies; and

★ To empower you to take positive action right away.

Each chapter title identifies a revolutionary success strategy, spelling out the acrostic [I love this word!] "V.I.C.T.O.R.Y."

V	VISION
I	INTEL
C	COACHING
T	TEAM BUILDING
O	OPERATIONS
R	RAPID ACTION
Y	YOU

Each chapter contains:

★ **Key Challenge**: Over the years, I have had the good fortune to interview, mentor/coach, mastermind with, and learn from hundreds of other entrepreneurs. From these experiences I have distilled down key challenges that almost all entrepreneurs face at various times in starting and growing their businesses.

★ **Success Strategy:** The titles of Chapters 1 through 7 describe the revolutionary, battle-tested solutions (based on real-world experience—not theory) for dealing with each key challenge. **Developing Your VICTORY Success Plan** (Chapter 8) provides a step-by-step formula to create your action plan for VICTORY Success, regardless of the current stage of your business. My mastermind clients and educational seminar participants routinely tell me that this **VICTORY Success Plan** is the BEST business planning process they've ever used.

★ **E-Insights:** These short sidebars contain critical tips for recognizing and navigating the business minefields that can obstruct, delay, or adversely redirect even the most experienced entrepreneurs.

★ **Action Step:** These are short-focus exercises designed to help you *immediately implement* the key strategies of *Vision, Intel, Coaching, Team Building, Operations/Systems, Rapid Action* and *You.*

These exercises are *specifically designed* to help you step back and clearly see the broader picture of your business—and your own internal strengths—then quickly take appropriate positive action.

How to Use This Book

If You're An Aspiring Entrepreneur or in Start Up Mode
Read the entire book! Read it cover to cover, without skipping around, and complete the recommended **Action Step** exercises and assessments. This will help give you the bird's eye view—a 360° perspective that's often missing when you're swamped in the middle of starting and building your business. After that, carefully review the **Learn More** chapter at the end of this book. This will enable you to take full advantage of the powerful tools and support systems available for today's forward-thinking entrepreneurs.

If Your Business Is Already Running
If you've hit a roadblock or have gotten bogged down in business quicksand, you may want to use this book differently. First skim through and focus on the success strategies that really speak to you. After that, explore them fully and take decisive action. In my experience, business owners tend to become stuck or overwhelmed in a few key areas, and are too close to their own situation to clearly diagnose the problem. If this is you, think of this book as a toolkit: reach into it for the tool you need and take the appropriate course-corrective action to keep your business firing on all cylinders.

Before You Get Started

I know you're getting excited about the principles you'll find in this book. That's great—you should be! They will help you move your business closer to its fullest potential.

But before you keep reading, I'd like you to take a very important short detour. It's not required, but if you're as committed to the success of your business as I am, you'll find my suggestion to be absolutely essential. The businesses and lives of my coaching clients have been transformed by taking this detour; and every manager and leader in my hotel company has done the same.

Entrepreneurs enjoy the most success when they understand *themselves* (how they're built), as well as their businesses. For that reason, I'd ask that you start out by using a couple of powerful personal assessment tools I've found to help you better understand who you are and the unique strengths you possess. Burn-out, frustration and depression are often the result of working outside our unique strengths, so why not take an hour out of our lives to determine our inherent greatness?

The *Kolbe A Index* is an online assessment tool that will show you how you operate naturally in a given situation. It will also show you how you can use your innate Method of Operation in order to be more productive. The better you understand what you do best, the more you can incorporate your personal strengths into successful operation.

StrengthsFinder 2.0 is a book (and an online assessment tool) that will help you uncover your five inherent strengths. Many of us spend too much time doing things we are not naturally gifted to do. *StrengthsFinder 2.0* will help you connect to your talents, so you can invest your time and energy doing what you do best. If you don't want to read the entire book, we highly encourage you to take the online assessment and then read the five descriptions relevant to your indicated strengths.

These assessments do not take long to complete; the knowledge you gain about yourself will prove invaluable in applying the principles in this book to your business. Invest the time to do them right now! You can find links to both the _Kolbe A Index_ and _StrengthsFinders 2.0_ in the **Learn More** chapter of this book. Once you've completed these crucial assessments, you're ready to dive into the VICTORY success strategies.

I'm excited you've decided to join me on the entrepreneurial journey! It's time to break the multi-generational chains of financial, emotional, mental and spiritual poverty that many of us have inherited and endured. It's time to grab these demons by the throat, and claim the life of significance, prosperity, and positive impact we deserve!

So let's get started!

CHAPTER 1

VISION

Without vision, the people will perish.

Proverbs 29:18

Would you like to build an outstanding organization, one that progresses from good to great and beyond? Then you *must* have a clearly articulated vision to guide you and your team.

In this chapter, we'll look at the importance of developing a clear vision for your business—a vision built upon and reflective of your own principles—and how to define and communicate your vision for maximum benefit.

Key Challenge

Many entrepreneurs lack a clear understanding of who they aspire to become, and what they (and their companies) are truly capable of accomplishing. They haven't yet realized the full positive impact their ideas can have on their families, clients, and the broader community. This is because they haven't yet learned to apply their own unique strengths, abilities, and core values—the very things that form the foundation of sustainable success—to find their guiding vision for personal *and* business success. **You won't get far without a clear vision!**

But here's something that may surprise you: you actually **can** operate a reasonably successful business without a clear vision. Every day, we use products and services provided by companies that don't have a vision statement. It's true! You absolutely can achieve a certain level of success in business without a vision for your organization. The thing is, it's a real challenge to navigate the turbulent waters of economic downturns, sustainable business growth, or key personnel changes **without** a clearly articulated vision.

Vision without action is a daydream.
Action with without vision is a nightmare.
— Japanese Proverb

Vision is the most important strategy for achieving *enduring* success in business

My own experience, combined with the experience of other successful entrepreneurs I've studied, clearly shows that wildly successful organizations all share several common characteristics. Chief among them is a clear vision of where they are going and exactly what "success" means for them.

Let's be crystal clear about this: vision is the most important strategy for achieving enduring success in business. Long-term, sustainable success will evade you unless you possess a clear vision of where you're going as an organization—and as a person. It will, however, take a little bit of effort for some, and considerable heavy lifting for others, to distill, define, and disseminate your vision. If that sounds like it's too much of a pain to bother with and you're content with mediocrity, feel free to set this book down and keep doing things like you always have ... the rest of us are moving forward!

Why is vision so important? Because it allows you, as a leader, to spell communicate your ideas, goals, and aspirations. This means more than just physical, quantifiable goals. Your company vision should reflect your own core values—the fundamental principles you've chosen to guide everything you do in life. Vision is a compass that defines your culture, keeping you and your team on course towards your aspirational goals, maintaining positive momentum, and inspiring all key stakeholders through the challenges entrepreneurs go through at every level of business.

One of my favorite sayings is, *"Only those who can see the invisible can do the impossible."* A clear vision helps you see the unseen; it helps you discover what's possible. Running your business—or your life, for that matter—without a vision or mission statement is like taking a road trip without a map: it burns up a *lot* of fuel, and you might not even reach your destination!

This chapter opens with the quote *"without vision, the people will perish."* Many entrepreneurs don't understand the truth—the reality—of this statement. They undervalue the importance of vision. It's their loss! They're missing the sense of direction vision provides for their entire team.

Without vision, a.k.a. your entrepreneurial compass, your business is likely to veer off-course when trouble strikes. You'll sail all over the sea seeking solutions. You might try one thing today, and something else tomorrow, with nothing really coming together.

Disclosure: I have already made virtually every mistake that can possibly be made in business. In fact, I believe that to achieve success, you *need* to make a lot of mistakes! (It is, after all, one of the quickest ways to learn.) One of the most important reasons to have a crystal-clear vision is that when you *do* make a mistake, your vision helps you get back on track quickly and efficiently

It's all too easy to chase after quick fixes and silver bullets that will allegedly solve all your problems. Imagine the inevitable for every business: the economy starts to tank, revenue starts to slide, competitors open shop right across the street, or you're going through personnel challenges. Now more than ever, you need to know what's important to you. You need to know where you want your business to go. If you don't, you may find yourself cutting corners or even compromising your ethics "just this one time" to get things back on track. And that's a slippery slope.

With a clear vision, you won't end up spinning out of control, hoping to find your way when you hit a rough patch. You can get right back on track, without wasting valuable time on trial and error. When you keep vision—your destination—in mind, it always guides you back to what's important for the journey and what's essential to your business.

A clear vision is your battle cry, your call to action!

Vision means asking yourself the all-important question, *"What am I trying to achieve?"* and then taking the appropriate steps to move forward in that direction.

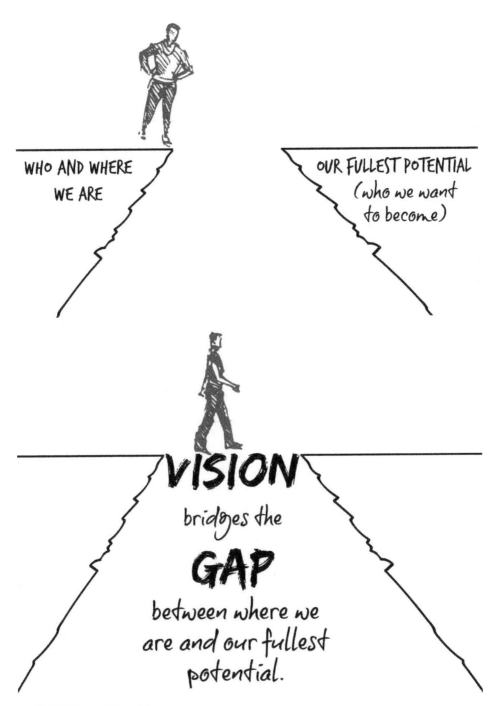

WHO AND WHERE
WE ARE

OUR FULLEST POTENTIAL
(who we want
to become)

VISION

bridges the

GAP

between where we
are and our fullest
potential.

Vision is the promise of what you will one day become. Your personal and professional vision statement should excite and prove to be a resource to refuel, recharge, and re-energize your efforts. A vision that inspires greatness is both positive and inspirational, defining what life *could* be. An awesome vision statement will inspire you every time you read it, attract superstars to join you on your quest, and serve as a guide to shape future decisions to grow your life and business.

Vision also provides you with the *fuel* you need to keep moving forward. A clearly-defined vision motivates you to keep going. When you have what James Collins and Jerry Porras, authors of *Built to Last*, call a "BHAG" (Big Hairy Audacious Goal), your vision generates motivation, movement, and momentum.

Vision is an appeal to our better selves to become something more. Clear vision has provided the motivation for history's greatest advances. Just look at the great explorers—Columbus, Magellan, Lewis and Clark—they each had a vision of what could be, of what they could accomplish. They fantasized about what lay beyond the horizon. Their vision motivated them and propelled them forward into the unknown, and it moved them and their teams, guiding them towards their goals. As an entrepreneur, you are just like these explorers: you must have a vision of what the future can be.

A clear vision is your battle cry, your call to action. It enables you to attract the best people—the "rock stars"—of your industry, inspiring team members to give their best and igniting creativity. Your vision, your *idea*, is an aspiration to a bigger, better future; being part of something larger than oneself is a prime motivator for many top performers.

A clear and compelling vision also attracts savvy investors. Countless companies have attracted investors and sizable rounds of equity infusion (even before the company launch or the realization of profitability) because of the clearly articulated vision by the Founder.

Your vision also helps you connect with your company's most loyal clients— your dedicated fans. In the next two sections, we'll examine the ways your vision can affect your employees (we call them "team members" in my organizations) and your customers (though I prefer to call them clients, as customers are transitional and clients are relational), as well as how you can develop your own vision for your business.

Here are the vision statements of a few well-known companies ... note how simple some are:

★ Apple, Inc. Vision Statement: *Apple is committed to bringing the best personal computing experience to students, educators, creative professionals and consumers around the world through its innovative hardware, software, and internet offerings.*

★ Google, Inc. Vision Statement: *To organize the world's information and make it universally accessible and useful.*

★ Coca-Cola **Enterprises, Inc. Vision Statement:** *Our vision serves as the framework for our Roadmap and guides every aspect of our business by describing what we need to accomplish in order to continue achieving sustainable, quality growth.*
  - *People: Be a great place to work where people are inspired to be the best they can be.*
  - *Portfolio: Bring to the world a portfolio of quality beverage brands that anticipate and satisfy people's desires and needs.*

- ***Partners:*** *Nurture a winning network of customers and suppliers, together we create mutual, enduring value.*
- ***Planet:*** *Be a responsible citizen that makes a difference by helping build and support sustainable communities.*
- ***Profit:*** *Maximize long-term return to shareowners while being mindful of our overall responsibilities.*
- ***Productivity:*** *Be a highly effective, lean and fast-moving organization.*

The soul becomes dyed with the color of its thoughts.
— *Marcus Aurelius*

Communicating a clear vision will dramatically affect your business

Outstanding organizations *always* have vision statements. The leaders of these organizations know that these statements must be well-defined and effectively communicated to their team members. Your team includes *all* the stakeholders in your business: investors, vendors, team members, and clients. You need all the people who are essential to your company's success to get on board with your vision, and to do that, they need to understand it.

By effectively communicating your vision, you keep your team members inspired and empower them to make decisions that are in line with your own ideas. Many entrepreneurs tell me the same story: they have difficulty managing their teams. Team members keep interrupting them, asking the same questions over and over again, because they're afraid to make decisions.

Situations like this are a strong sign that there is a problem in conveying the company's vision. Usually, team members don't know what the vision is for the organization. If they don't have your destination in mind, how will they plot your course? In organizations where every person understands the vision—both the core values and the hard, tangible goals— team members are able to make effective, appropriate decisions by themselves. The company's vision—your idea—is *their* compass, too, helping them navigate even in uncharted waters.

When you can clearly communicate your vision, you will be able to connect with your clients on a deeper level. In fact, you may end up creating clients who are also huge fans of your business. A great example of this is Apple, Inc. They stayed true to their vision, even though for decades they lagged behind their competition in terms of worldwide market share in the PC and mobile device industry.

Their vision was to provide a very user-friendly interface. They built products that were simple enough for anyone to use, even without a degree in technology. Staying true to that vision has definitely paid off. If you look at Apple over the past couple of decades, they've made huge strides by pulling traditional business users into the Mac universe and creating devices that people love and adore.

They kept pursuing their vision to make devices that people love for their functionality and ease of use. As a result, they developed a fiercely loyal client base—the kind of clients who will save an organization during difficult times. The rest of the computer industry is playing catch-up.

★ E-INSIGHT ★

Clearly Communicating Your Vision Attracts Rock Star Team Members!

I found this to be true in my hospitality company, broughtonHOTELS. I started my company with a clearly defined vision, and I was able to succinctly articulate that vision. That gave me the ability to attract top-notch hospitality people to work with me.

In the early days of our organization, I hired industry rock stars who could have worked anywhere they chose. Some of my new team members were asked by friends and industry colleagues, "Why are you working for this Broughton guy? He's only got two small hotels! You should be a COO or CFO someplace else!" The reason I could hire such great people was because they bought into my vision of growing an extraordinary organization far beyond our current stage. They knew I wanted to build a world-class hospitality organization based on innovation and accessibility, and a work environment that embraced honesty, authenticity, and integrity. My vision resonated with them. They got it, and wanted to change the industry with me.

Have you ever been to an Apple Store? It's usually busy, regardless of the time of day. The stores aren't much to look at, yet people flock there to spend their money on Apple products and get hands-on training from knowledgeable trainers who help them learn how to make the most of their technology purchase. By contrast, other computer companies, like Dell and Gateway, opened retail stores with little success. The stores were usually empty, poorly staffed, and ultimately abandoned for a multi-line reseller model.

What set Apple apart? Their customers bought into the company's vision and they became very loyal clients. In fact, team members there don't really need to push for sales. They simply help people: they provide information, answer questions, demo products, and empower people to make decisions.

Chick-fil-A, founded by Truett Cathy, is another example of a company that attracts both customers and team members because of its vision. They have a waiting list of people who want to be operator/partners to open new stores with them because people understand and subscribe to their vision. Even before they begin working for the organization, they know they want to work for Chick-fil-A because of the values the company has defined.

By having a clearly defined vision, Chick-fil-A attracts leading entrepreneurs and food industry people up and down the corporate ladder. The company puts a high priority on its people having quality time with their families, so Chick-fil-A goes against the grain. While every other quick-service restaurant remains open on Sundays, Chick-fil-A restaurants are always closed. But because they've attracted team members and customers who buy into the organization's vision, they produce more revenue on a per-unit basis in six days than anyone else in their segment does in seven days.

So, we've seen that a clear vision can give your company guidance and motivation. It can help attract top team members and investors in your industry. Plus, it can help you build a rabidly loyal client base. But, how do you discover your compelling vision, and communicate it effectively? I will answer those questions in the next section.

A goal without a plan is just a wish.
— Antoine de Saint-Exupery

You Must Be Clear and Passionate In Communicating Your Vision

Remember, we are talking about creating a vision for your business. I find that many entrepreneurs have a clear personal vision for their lives, but they haven't developed a clear vision for their businesses. You need to have a separate vision that applies specifically and directly to your company. Even though your personal values and core beliefs will be a big part of your company, you need a corporate vision that attracts and motivates your team members, and propels your business to a new level.

But what does it really mean to have vision? Close your eyes and imagine the look and feel of your world when your energy and efforts have served their ultimate purpose ... this is your vision. It's much bigger than words printed on stationery or a clever sign hung in the break room.

Creating a clear vision for your business can seem like a daunting task. The reality is that you will need to put in some time and brainpower to develop a vision. Sound a bit overwhelming? Don't worry! Just make sure you take the time to complete the **Action Step** exercise at the end of this chapter.

Your vision doesn't need to be complicated or earth shattering. In fact, the simpler it is, the more compelling it can be. Some strategic coaches even suggest you create a physical vision board or short video to capture the essence of the vision you have for both yourself and your company, and have them where you can see them every single day to keep the vision front and center. Equally important to the written mantra is playing the mental movie, by visualizing the journey and the attainment of your goals. If you don't believe it's possible and can't visualize it, how will you inspire and enlist others to join your cause? Olympians, warriors, peacemakers, and empire builders have all used the power of visualization to achieve their goals. Here's how:

- ★ Step 1: Create an inspiring vision.
- ★ Step 2: Believe it!
- ★ Step 3: Visualize every detail of what success looks like, sounds like, feels like, and smells like.
- ★ Step 4: Take action to make it so.

When the going gets tough and you feel discouraged, play the movie in your mind to remind yourself of where you are going. This will help you refocus on how good the rewards will feel once your company accomplishes them.

One of the most compelling examples of the power of a clear vision comes from two-time Olympic gold medalist Brian Goodell. During his swimming career, Brian earned five world records and received the Congressional Medal of Achievement, among other honors. *Sports Illustrated* called him the personification of discipline and hard work.

But his career almost didn't end up that way. Today I'm fortunate to call Brian my friend, and every time I hear him recount his experience of his first Olympic event, I get chills. He had trained for the Olympics for four years, from the age of 13. Expectations were high for winning not just a medal, but a gold medal. And then things started to go terribly wrong. Here's Brian in his own words:

Brian Goodell's Olympic Vision

My first event in Olympic games in Montreal was the 1,500-meter freestyle. It was the day after the opening ceremony. And before that race started, when I was in warm up, I started to get some butterflies. As the pre-race introductions progressed, I was so nervous that when they called us to the blocks I realized I couldn't feel my arms or my legs.

So, the race started and finally as I got into the race I began to get into my comfort zone. I was in third place near the midpoint of the race, and going in to the final third of the race where you really have to go through a pain barrier. At that moment, I began to visualize the award ceremony which I had visualized thousands of times before with my affirmations and my goal cards, and when I was swimming and when I was sleeping, and when I was in class in high school. And that picture didn't match up, because in this case, in the picture, I was standing on the third level getting the bronze medal, and the picture that I had held so tight and programmed in my mind was the gold medal. And something inside said 'no way!' and I started to be able to reach a little further in front, push the water further behind.

At that moment, I could separate the pain, and the gasping for air, and the oxygen debt. I could separate that from my mind which was, I could just be the pilot pushing the controls to the full.

I learned visualization and affirmations in 1975, and did them on a daily basis to build up confidence in my mind, and also to help me perform and practice, to play Olympics in practice is really what I did on a daily basis, so that by the time I went to the Olympic trials in 1976, I knew I was going to win my events. I knew I was going to break the world records. And I did that.

Brian not only came from behind to win the gold medal, he set a new world record, which held for four years. Brian's visualization was so detailed, he says it played like a movie in his mind. He pictured himself on the gold medal podium, he could feel the weight of the gold medal around his neck and he could see the flag being raised, hear the national anthem. He attributes his Olympic performances to both his physical preparation and his mental visualizations, and today inspires young swimmers and performers with his experience.

You will need to revisit this process several times, until you create a vision you can commit to pursuing. Although your vision should be one that stretches and inspires your company to higher heights, it should be realistic. If you develop a vision that is too idealistic or overly optimistic, it is guaranteed that your team members will become frustrated. The real test of an articulated vision is whether your team and supporters understand what it takes to bring it to life, and whether they're equipped to take action to make it so. Be certain it's a vision people will be proud to be part of, either as a team member or as a client.

Your vision needs to represent your core values in a very direct way. It's important for your vision to be crystal clear, authentic, and unapologetic. You don't want to be confrontational. You just want to say, "This is who we are, this is what we believe, and this is why. If that sounds good to you, we would love to do business with you. If you don't resonate with it, that's great. There are hundreds or thousands of other businesses out there with which you could be happy. But this is who we are. This is how we roll."

Be crystal clear, authentic, and unapologetic.

Once you have developed a vision you, your team members, and your clients want to take ownership of, it's time to communicate it. You want people to understand it, see the possibilities in it, and themselves as part of it. For that to happen, you must be clear about what the vision is. Rehearse it in your head. Think about it often. When you are sure you have a clear picture of the vision, you will be able to share it with others.

The key to communicating your vision to others is to make sure it is communicated clearly and repeatedly. For most of the entrepreneurs I know, the most effective way to communicate vision is verbally. Talk about your vision with everyone you do business with—team members, vendors, customers, anyone—so that everyone understands who you are and what your company is about.

Consider different ways to keep your vision in front of you and your team members and stakeholders, such as hanging a copy of your vision statement at every entrance at work, putting it in a prominent spot on your website, commissioning a mural or infographic that captures its essence, or featuring it prominently on your letterhead or in your email signature block.

Enterprise-Rent-A-Car has a copy of its company's "cultural compass" hanging in each office where both customers and team members will see it. Likewise, Aveda Spas display a beautifully printed and framed copy of their mission statement in the lounge area where their clients can read it. The more often you and your team repeat your vision, the more ingrained it becomes in everyone's thinking.

Why do you need to repeat your vision often? You repeat it often because when you are dealing with the day-to-day business details (cutting checks, controlling inventory, managing team member issues, making payroll, etc.)—dealing with vendors, with production people, and with customers—it's easy to lose sight of why you are in business (for both you and your team members).

When you communicate your vision often, it reminds everybody: "Hey, this is why we do this. This is why we get out of bed every day."

Larry Yatch's Sealed Mindset

Larry Yatch served for ten years as an officer in the elite U.S. Navy SEAL teams. He was medically retired after being critically injured in the line of duty. Then Larry started his own business, to redirect his expertise and unique skills and knowledge to help others with a leadership mindset, and personal safety.

Larry participated in one of my mastermind sessions several years ago and just prior to his spotlight session he shared with the group that for all the combat missions and stressful situations he had experiences as a SEAL, "the scariest and most difficult thing I ever did was launch and run my own business." He said his vision for how his business would positively impact his family, life, and legacy propelled him to persevere and drive on.

If a decorated Navy SEAL like Larry Yatch says the entrepreneurial path is a difficult one, perhaps we should believe it! When the going gets tough, our clearly articulated, inspiring vision reminds us and our teammates who we are, what we do, and why we exist.

If you need more inspiration for your vision statement, consider these visions from your fellow entrepreneurs:

★ *To bring inspiration and innovation to every athlete in the world.* — Nike (founded by Phil Knight)

★ *To be one of the world's most innovative full-service hospitality management and development companies by inspiring significance and distinction for our guests, associates, and communities.* — broughtonHOTELS (founded by Larry Broughton)

★ *Creating solutions to enable consumers of all fitness levels to unlock their body's potential.* — Perfect Fitness (founded by Alden Mills)

★ *Our absolutely, positively spirit puts our customers at the heart of everything we do.* — FedEx Service Statement (founded by Fred Smith)

How will the vision for *your* company inspire, challenge and motivate?

People want and need something to aspire to. They want to be part of something greater than themselves. When you present your team members with a vision of the great things the team can accomplish together, you give them a chance to be part of something bigger. This will be especially attractive to high achievers, who love to be challenged.

★ VICTORY SUCCESS STORY ★

I was just starting to think about a business when I got my hands on the first edition of VICTORY. *I had worked for a number of years in a full-time job which provided stability, but not creativity. I was newly divorced and had just finished my college degree in psychology. I found that within the entrepreneur world there was this opportunity to create something. It took several months learning what kind of business I would actually do. It's been a journey!*

Tammi Moses
Chief Encouragement Officer
Homes are for Living, LLC

Then in December 2013, I met Larry at a conference for women military veteran entrepreneurs. I had to submit an application with a proposal of what kind of business I wanted to start, just to be accepted to attend the conference. I didn't really know yet what I was going to do. I was interested in housing and homelessness and trying to resolve some of those issues.

As a result of reading and working through the exercises in VICTORY, *and working with Larry in his mentoring group, I came to the idea that I should talk about hoarding issues because of my experience growing up that way. There was a real need for understanding in that arena. I'm so close to the issue that I couldn't fathom it was something I could turn into a business!*

For me, vision starts with figuring out what it is you're trying to accomplish and thinking, "what kind of impact do I want to have?" I have no idea what my original vision statement was, but I'm sure it was a page long or more. Larry's advice helped me bring it down to something more succinct that doesn't bore people or confuse them.

The result now has finally boiled down to providing positive hoarding solutions as a Chief Encouragement Officer. That's my whole objective: to be positive, provide solutions, and encourage people. Whether I'm working with people who are hoarding or not, have a little bit of clutter, or are overwhelmed, they just need a little bit of encouragement to make a different choice to change their outcome.

VICTORY *helped me take a step back from, "I'm going to do this or I'm going to do that," and it made me realize what a big impact I could have if I let myself do that and get out of my own way. As a person, I have become much more transparent in why I do what I do and how I came to it. I have decided that I am the voice of adult kids who hoard and what I have found by feeling the fear and doing it anyway, and just being brave and saying, "Hey, I know about this issue." People resonate with it, whether I'm sponsoring a booth at a landlords' conference or speaking at a housing fair. I'm convinced of the power of a clear, simple, and strong vision.*

Now, it's your turn! Share your *VICTORY* success story with me at success@larrybroughton.me. I'd love to hear from you!

A leader has the vision and conviction that a dream can be achieved.
He inspires the power and energy to get it done.
— Ralph Lauren

★ ACTION STEP: DEFINE YOUR VISION ★

Get ready to take action! Take some time to begin the process of developing a vision for your business. Don't rush it … this is a critical component for enduring success.

Here's a simple, two-step process you can use to help you develop your company's vision. (If you'd like to use this book as your notebook, I've included some notes pages at the end of each chapter.)

Step 1: Begin by spending about 15 minutes identifying your personal core values. Write down three people you admire, then under each person write down three characteristics you admire about them. Circle anything they have in common. These are values with which you naturally resonate. Use this list as a guideline to identify your own personal values.

Step 2: Now, take an additional 30 uninterrupted minutes alone. Find a secluded spot to slow your mind, reflect, and then think. Think about who you are, and what's important to you as the leader of this company. Think about the things you would like to see your business accomplish in the years ahead. It's helpful to think about what you want to see your company do in the short-term (the next one, three, and five years), and the long-term (ten years and beyond).

Don't be too critical of yourself at this early stage of the process. You'll very likely need to come back to revisit this process several times before you're satisfied you have adequately captured a vision for what it means for your business to be successful. Once you've got it, formally revisit it each year (perhaps on the company anniversary) to ask yourself and your team if you're still on track, or whether it needs to be modified. The vision for your organization should be both inspirational and aspirational; declaring who you aspire to be, not necessarily who you are today.

While you're reflecting, jot down some notes, phrases, and adjectives that come to mind. Imagine what success and life feels like once your company has accomplished its goals. Visualizing images of completed goals, and tapping into their associated emotions, holds tremendous power.

If you get really stuck, ask yourself these important questions:

★ How many people can I help when I achieve my vision?

★ Who will benefit when I achieve my vision?

★ What will the positive impact on my life be when I achieve my vision?

Before you start the next chapter, take action and start crafting your inspirational and aspirational vision statement. I promise, you won't regret doing this!

_____

_____

_____

_____

_____

_____

_____

_____

_____

_____

_____

_____

_____

_____

_____

_____

_____

CHAPTER 2

INTEL

Victorious warriors win first and then go to war, while defeated warriors go to war first and then seek to win.

Sun Tzu

ntelligence: *the gathering of key information and insights to gain a competitive advantage.* That's not a dictionary definition, but it's highly accurate in the business sense. This chapter will guide you through the process of gathering, analyzing, and using intel to help your business succeed.

Key Challenge

One surefire way to *miss* your mark, in business or otherwise, is to jump into action without gathering all the background information you need to make informed decisions. This is especially true in business. Too many entrepreneurs are launching their ventures with incomplete insight into key areas that are essential for their short and long-term success.

Critical coverage points include (but are certainly not limited to): detailed knowledge of the market for your product or service, analysis of your current or potential competition, and assessment of the resources available to you.

Most importantly, many entrepreneurs lack understanding of their most important assets: their own strengths and weaknesses.

*An organization's ability to learn, and translate that learning into
action rapidly, is the ultimate competitive advantage.*
— Jack Welch

Thorough Intelligence is Essential to Realize Your True Vision

How important is intel? You probably know the story of Lieutenant Colonel George Armstrong Custer and how he learned this the hard way. At the Battle of Little Big Horn in 1876, he failed to appreciate the size, power, and *resolve* of the Native American forces he faced. As a result, he foolishly divided his own forces, failed to make adequate provisions for ammunition and supplies, and launched multiple uncoordinated and non-supporting attacks against a numerically superior and equally armed opponent.

We all know what happened because Custer acted without first understanding his situation.

If you're going to lead your company to the level you envision, you absolutely *must* do your homework—diligently acquire the information you need and make sure you understand it. Let's be crystal-clear on this important point: *you cannot lead a successful organization without proper intel!*

Only by filling the big-picture view with detailed, accurate data in developing your business vision will you enable your team to achieve that vision successfully.

You cannot lead a successful organization without proper intel.

In **Vision** (Chapter 1), you learned how a focused vision is vital to the success of your business. Now you know that without reliable intel, you won't even know if achieving that vision is possible. Some important questions you should keep in mind throughout this chapter include:

- ★ What key points of information do I need to make my decisions?
- ★ What resource(s) do I need to obtain that intelligence and analyze it effectively?
- ★ What systems do I need to regularly confirm that the information I am relying on is valid and relevant to where I am, right now, in business?

The first things that spring to most peoples' minds when they hear "intel" are war movies and spy novels (or vice versa). It's actually a pretty good analogy for entrepreneurship, but in the business context, "intel" means gathering information about your market, your own organization and your competitors. OK, it's not as sexy, fun, or exciting as your favorite clandestine adventure (which is exactly why many entrepreneurs don't like to do it), but it is critical to driving your ideas forward.

Let's be honest. If you're like most entrepreneurs (including me), you're an action-oriented being. You want to get out there and make things *happen*; your energy comes from getting things *done*. The whole idea of sitting down and doing research, analyzing with the resources you need, or just finding out what those resources are can be a challenge and a major energy drain for us.

Another common disconnect is many entrepreneurs find it easier to *talk* about vision than to gather information to support it. Many of us are "big picture" people, and collecting intel is, by its nature, micro-detail-oriented. But the rewards for committing to the sometimes-tedious work of gathering intel— and, by the way, ***doing what most of your potential competitors won't***—are well worth it.

Sometimes entrepreneurs miss the importance of things like intel and developing vision because, frankly, they're not covered in the resources that are most readily available to us. Often those who are either just starting a business or wanting to expand their existing business turn to classes or programs offered through the SBA.

Remember, I believe that the people who run these programs really *do* mean well, as stated in the Introduction to this book. But my experience—and the experience of scores of others I've interviewed—is that many would-be entrepreneurs come out of these classes and counseling programs more confused and less confident in their own abilities than they were when they started.

Few of the successful entrepreneurs I've talked to count the SBA among the resources they've used as a key part of their success. In fact, it ends up being more of a hindrance in many cases. Why? Because their focus isn't pertinent in today's business world. Developing an exhaustive, old-school, dust-collecting, 6-inch-thick business plan, seeking traditional sources of financing that are very hard to come by (especially for innovative, but unproven, business ideas), and building a traditional, staff-heavy, bricks-and-mortar operation is simply not the effective model it once was.

The keys to your success are not found in some slick business plan. They will be found in the things I talk about in this book (after all, unlike many of those directing and conducting old school business classes, I've *actually used* these principles, and witnessed scores of others do the same, to build and grow successful organizations). I'm not discounting the value of an action-oriented, user-driven business plan. Rather, I'm saying there is a right way and a wrong way to create one. You need to focus on vision, core values, mindset and, of course, good intel. These are the *real* foundations for your long-term success.

> ## The keys to your success are not found in some slick business plan.

Since accurate intelligence is so vital to your success, let's explore in detail how you can gather it, and what to do with the information once you've got it. The good news? This is the best time ever to obtain solid intel on your target industry. Information that, barely a decade ago, cost thousands (or even tens of thousands) of dollars to access through proprietary information gatekeepers is now readily available with a little bit of Internet savvy and a couple of mouse clicks.

It's easier (and cheaper) than ever before to acquire the information you need when exploring whether your business idea is viable. Getting the tools you need to develop and market your business and building virtual teams to drastically lower ongoing business costs is more convenient, and you've now got multiple channels for directly engaging your ideal client or customer. Unfortunately, this easy access to information is also a curse, since the sheer volume of information available means you'll need to sift through a lot of silt to get to the gold … it can be truly exhausting.

The ability to know whether your idea can be successful is really at the heart of gathering intel. Discovering that there *is* a place for your idea—that people want it, and that you can carve out a spot for yourself in the market—gives you the confidence to plunge ahead. Contrarily, if you find that your idea may not work in its current context, you've already generated the information you need to refine your approach (or to move on to another idea altogether).

No matter what you discover, intel is a critical first step in realizing your vision. So, what are the best approaches to gathering the information you need?

What's the use of running if you are not on the right road?
— German Proverb

Intel Is Like Homework—
With the Key Being "Work"

At first glance, you wouldn't think it would be that tough, because in its simplest form, business intel includes just three things:

★ Gathering information;

★ Processing and analyzing that information; and

★ Disseminating and acting on that information.

Of course, the first part—the gathering—is much easier to do if you're working in a field in which you've already gained significant experience and contacts. In this case, you should connect with and leverage the resources you already have: your own experience, your current associates or colleagues, your former colleagues, former bosses, and managers, and your circle(s) of industry contacts.

If you're starting out fresh in a new industry, it's more of a challenge. So where do you begin? Start by taking the big picture view of your particular industry. This macro perspective helps you see the broad outline of your industry and find answers to key questions, such as:

★ How large is the market?

★ What are the developing trends?

★ Who are the major players?

★ What are the opportunities and pitfalls?

Almost every industry has at least one trade or professional association; these can be valuable sources of initial information. These associations exist to provide people with facts and statistics about their specific industry, provide continuing education and connect businesses with their clients/customers and suppliers. Once you've got the big picture and really understand the industry, you can start painting a detailed picture of your own business. Trade associations are a great place to start, but you'll need more intel to know for sure whether your idea has what it takes to fly.

★ E-INSIGHT ★

Get Experience in Your Industry

Throughout this chapter, I stress the value of developing relationships with experienced people in your industry to benefit from the collective wisdom of those who have "been there, done that." Many otherwise smart business owners try to reinvent the wheel instead of taking advantage of the value of learning from seasoned pros.

If you are new to a particular industry, a great way to gain hands-on experience is to get a job working for someone else in that industry for a year or two (or to pursue an internship, especially if you have gone back to school). I know many of you just recoiled at the thought of getting a J.O.B. and working for someone else. I can assure you, however, that working on the front lines, or in the trenches of a new industry, is one of the quickest ways to learn the ins and outs of a new industry. In most cases, spending your time on the front lines in a new industry is far more valuable than theoretical case studies in a sterile academic environment.

An excellent alternative is to partner with someone who has direct experience in your industry and who can act as a formal or informal advisor. Building such a relationship with a trusted mentor offers multiple advantages, including networking, support, and experience.

I strongly recommend to my mastermind members to put together a Board of Advisors. The ones who do see more expansion in their business and recognize their blind spots more easily. It can be a small group, even just three people, who are further along the path than you and who have been where you are. Cast a wide net and find people in your industry who are where you want to be. Look for people who augment your weaknesses and share your ethos, and who will be invested in your success.

The abundance of data available today in any given industry is simply mind-blowing. Not all "facts" are created equally, so you'll need to separate the relevant from the irrelevant and the "actionable intel" from the "nice to know" fluff.

Here are some sources for good intel:

- ★ Industry news reports
- ★ Speeches given by key industry thought leaders
- ★ The presentation program or agenda for industry meetings or trade shows
- ★ Anything else that provides a clear picture of what's hot

This may not be fun, exciting work, but the payoffs can be huge! In your research, you're likely to unearth a few choice nuggets of information that'll make all the difference to your business. You might discover an underserved niche or identify an emerging trend that you can enter on the ground floor. Often, existing industry players are too entrenched to even see the opportunity or aren't nimble enough to capitalize on a new trend. This allows fresh eyes and new ideas to make an immediate impact, because you *can* "see the forest for the trees." Great examples of maverick companies who've disrupted traditional, entrenched industries are Uber and Air BnB.

If you have ever worked in a large, hide-bound organization, you know that making even the smallest change is kind of like turning a battleship around in a bathtub. This is why opportunities to repackage or reposition current industry offerings or quickly take advantage of an industry-wide blind spot occur quite frequently.

★ E-INSIGHT ★

Interview the Experts!

I cannot stress enough the importance of consulting experts in your industry. Some things are learned only after you immerse yourself in an area of study for a number of years.

The "10,000 Hour Rule" (based on the research of Dr. K. Anders Ericsson and popularized by author Malcolm Gladwell in his best-selling book *Outliers: The Story of Success*) holds that it takes a minimum of 10,000 hours of study and practice to achieve mastery in a subject or profession (about 20 hours a week for ten years). You need to schedule time with people who have superior experience and wisdom, and ask them to share what they've learned.

You're probably wondering, "aren't these people too busy to talk to me?" The answer is, in many cases, no!

Successful people often look for opportunities to give back, to improve the industry that has been so good to them. They will often give you an appointment so you can ask questions, if you follow a few simple rules:

* ★ Rule #1 - Be specific
* ★ Rule #2 - Be respectful of their time
* ★ Rule #3 - Be thankful

Don't forget to thank them with a handwritten note or small thank you gift. Look for ways to develop a long-term relationship, such as sending them a note when their company gets a big contract or is featured in a news story.

Want to shorten your learning curve and gain a deeper perspective in a short amount of time? Seek out and connect with industry leaders: the people who are keynoting industry events, having articles published about them, receiving awards for innovation, and challenging the status quo. Study them, learn what they're doing and how they're doing it. Reach out to request an informational meeting; find out where they think the industry is headed.

You might be thinking, "but why would somebody that important give me the time of day?"

If you approach them from a place of genuine curiosity and with a humble spirit, you'll find that many top industry leaders are happy to answer your questions. Many are passionate about creating change within their industry, and that change often comes from fresh perspective or new blood. It's true, even with people you think are too busy to talk to you. But if you do get turned down (and it happens), suck it up and move on to the next person.

Most people love filling the role of a mentor or guru, and you should take every advantage of this fact. Just remember to always be respectful of that person's time and energy, and to give back. You want to build mutually beneficial relationships with leaders in your industry. You can only do that if you are willing to contribute—to give, as well as receive, support.

In the **Action Step** exercise at the end of this chapter, I suggest several important areas of your industry on which to focus your intel-gathering efforts.

But before that, I must stress one critically important area of intelligence that many smart, dedicated entrepreneurs still overlook: discovering whether your clients/customers actually *want* your product or service!

This may sound absurdly simple, but if nobody *wants* your product (or they don't see a need for it), they won't buy it. You would be shocked at the number of times I've had entrepreneurs tell me they know exactly what their market *needs*, and how they are going to educate customers to change their perception (and make a fortune in the process). Following this path without confirming you are offering something people actually *want* is usually a quick ticket to the poorhouse.

Maybe your idea *is* completely revolutionary. It's exactly what people need, but you'd better pay attention to what people *want* and incorporate that into your product or service. Otherwise, no one is going to give you a chance—that means they'll never discover how great your product or service really is!

The problem is that when you try to tell people you have what they need, whether they want it or not, your audience often hears it as, "Hey! You are too dumb to know what's good for you. Let me tell you what you really need."

If nobody wants your product...
they won't buy it.

Nobody likes to be talked down to, and they'll immediately tune you out. Let's face it: if everyone did what they *needed* to do, we'd all be fit, rich, and married to Mr. or Mrs. Right! Don't assume you know something (like what your customers want or need) without checking it out, and if you are trying to sell something that "fixes" people (or companies), it is imperative to carefully craft your marketing message to solve a "*want*."

Let me give you the perfect example.

In the mid-1950s, Ford Motor Company decided to expand its offerings and created a new division to compete with General Motors' multiple lines. Ford spent more than two years developing this new car line, reportedly conducting thousands of surveys to create a car tailored to the desires and tastes of the American driver. Sounds like good intel so far, right?

Ford's ad agency spent months coming up with a name for the new brand, even sponsoring contests and hiring a well-known poet to brainstorm names. They tested numerous possibilities in polls across the country. But, when the chairman of the board saw the list of names (some reports say the ad men put forward 18,000 suggestions), the chairman said in exasperation, "Why don't we just call it 'Edsel'?" Maybe that was strike one—ignoring public opinion which had associated "Edsel" with words like "weasel" and "pretzel." (Edsel was the name of Henry Ford's son.)

Ford pressed on, and in the spring of 1957, the company mounted what was arguably the most successful pre-launch marketing campaign in history, driving up public curiosity—and expectations—like never before. In the summer of 1957, just weeks before the scheduled debut, the stock market plummeted. Ford ignored market reports that all car makers were ending their model years with record inventory (in other words, people weren't buying cars) and went ahead with their launch as planned.

On "E-Day," September 4, 1957, record numbers of ravenous fans showed up to Edsel showrooms across the country. But they didn't buy. The Edsel was a colossal failure—for many reasons, including operations, quality, and team morale—and I've often wondered what would have happened if they truly listened to the intel they so methodically (and I'd say expensively) gathered.

Gathering intel shows you exactly where your product or service fits in the overall scheme of the market. It also provides you the raw materials you'll need to build your plan of action for business success. Intel gathering is neither easy nor exciting, but it *is* absolutely necessary. Even the best information is worthless if it isn't used properly. Next, I'll share how to effectively analyze your intel and, more importantly, how to act on it.

Give me six hours to chop down a tree and
I will spend the first four sharpening the ax.
— Abraham Lincoln

Analyzing and Taking Action on the Intel You've Gathered

Just gathering information isn't enough. You must then take the time to analyze and understand this information to be able to use it to your advantage; to turn info into intel. You must develop a plan of action based on your analysis. And finally, you must take action!

One proven recipe for business disaster is attempting to analyze all the data

INTEL CYCLE

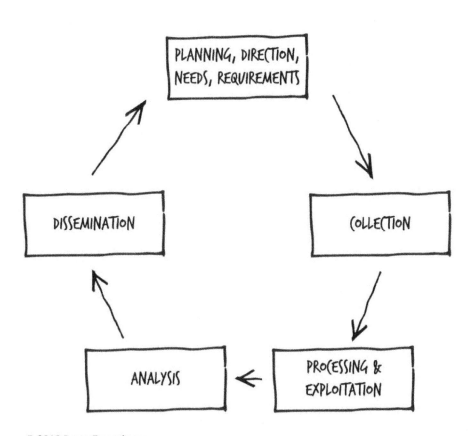

yourself. There's an old proverb that states, "plans go wrong for lack of advice; many advisors bring success."

As entrepreneurs, we sometimes develop blinders, or "tunnel vision," that allow us only to see things in a certain way. We get too close to our situations and lack the perspective to put all the pieces together in a way that makes sense. Therefore, we all need to define a group of people we can trust to give us their honest assessment and provide an alternate viewpoint when we get too fixated on a particular course of action—or inaction.

This is one of the merits of developing relationships with people who are bolder and brighter than ourselves. They often perceive things that we miss, either because we don't yet have the experience or because we are so focused on our "brilliant" idea that we aren't seeing clearly or understanding the bigger picture.

The saying, "none of us is as smart as all of us" is very true in business. Gather people you trust around you and enlist them to help you analyze and make sense of your intel. You will definitely discover more useful information than you would if you tried to do it all yourself.

For some entrepreneurs, the act of gathering intel isn't the issue (although it's still tedious work). Analyzing the data isn't even that difficult. Sometimes the biggest challenge can be *acting* upon what you learn. I believe the ability to take action is one of the key success factors separating exceptional entrepreneurs from mediocre ones. **Rapid Action** (Chapter 6) is devoted to developing this concept more fully.

The ability to take action is one of the key success factors.

If you want your intel to be *useful*, you've got to *do* something with it. You must get the relevant pieces of information to the people who need it—your team members, investors and key advisors, to start.

Want to put your banker to sleep? Load up your business plan with every fact you've uncovered. Want to confuse your team members? Drop a mountain of raw data on their desks without running it through your "vision" filter first and then expect them to work miracles with it.

You will quickly find that this is not the way to the success you've been dreaming of for so long. As the leader, visionary, and driver for your company, you are ultimately responsible for getting the right information into the right hands, providing strategic direction, and acting on your discoveries.

Once you've made your move, you may realize you've taken a wrong turn. What should you do? Move on! Take course-corrective action along the way. Chances are you're now smarter and wiser than before you started, and you're not likely to make the same mistake twice. Furthermore, don't beat yourself up over the mistakes you do make: you are going to make mistakes. Finally, whatever you do, do not listen to the naysayers who ask, "why don't you just get a real job?" or otherwise try to tear you down.

All entrepreneurs want to get their businesses off the ground smoothly. But with the first sign of resistance (or when they realize they're heading down the wrong road), some business owners become paralyzed. Frequently, this paralysis results in the inability to continue taking decisive action steps after making a big mistake. Just as often, fear comes as a result of running into some resistance; maybe from friends, family, industry experts, or even competitors.

They recoil from the pushback and sit there with their engine idling, going nowhere. Don't let this happen to you!

★ E-INSIGHT ★

Establish Relationships with Industry Leaders

Go beyond just meeting with industry experts – try to establish a more formal mentoring relationship with a recognized authority figure. As you learned in the previous E-Insight, successful people *enjoy* sharing their exciting discoveries. However, many people assume that they are unapproachable or—worse—only approach them from a position of "taking."

A more positive approach (and one boasting a much higher success rate) is coming from a place of service, either asking how you might be of service to them, or how you can support them in getting their message out. Be prepared to give generously, as you may have a skill or experience that your mentor finds valuable.

The biggest key is simply to ask! Even if you think someone is too big or too busy to mentor you, you need to ask if such a relationship is possible. Many entrepreneurs miss out on incredibly valuable opportunities because they fail to make the "big ask." Don't be one of them!

Every entrepreneur will have failures (trust me, I know from intimate, first-hand experience). Ben Franklin put it this way: "Success is moving from failure to failure without losing your enthusiasm."

And Soichiro Honda, the Japanese industrialist and founder of Honda Motor Company, famously said that "success is 99 percent failure." You need to maintain your confidence by focusing on your vision so you are able to recognize the one percent that makes a difference.

The reality is that every entrepreneur is going to make mistakes. It is crucial that you understand and believe in this concept, and not lose your enthusiasm or drive along the way.

However, the way you recover from a mistake or setback often makes all the difference between ultimate failure and success. My advice? When you realize you've made a mistake, reassess your strategy immediately, check your map, and get back to the right road—but this time with more reliable intel. You cannot let fear, embarrassment, or anything else keep you from taking immediate course-corrective action and forging ahead.

A critical corollary to my admonition above: do not fall so in love with your own brilliant ideas that you refuse to adjust your course or change tactics when necessary!

I find that this often occurs when you attempt to sell people what you think they need as opposed to what they want, as I discussed earlier in this chapter. Just to reinforce the point, you can avoid this by building a trusted team of advisors, mentors, and mastermind partners to assist you in analyzing, organizing, and vetting data before you take action on it. I'll explore this more in the next chapter.

Always remember, when we become too enamored with our own ideas, we tend to become very stubborn and entrenched in our own, sometimes limited, thinking.

★ VICTORY SUCCESS STORY ★

Travis McVey
Creator & Founder
Heroes Vodka

I got the spark of an idea for this business while sitting in a bar with some friends watching TV. It was around Veterans Day, and there was some ad paying lip service to giving back to our veterans. And I thought, I want to do something that will really give back to our heroes.

As a former U.S. Marine, I knew first hand the ultimate sacrifice that so many have made for our freedom, including one of my very good friends. That's what drove me to create Heroes Vodka. A portion of every sale is donated to a veteran-related charity, such as AMVETS.

At the time, I was working full-time for a tire company. I had been to business school and led teams, but I knew nothing about the vodka industry or starting a business. Through research, I learned that vodka outsold all other spirit categories combined, and that it was a very competitive business. So, although I started my company in 2009 and our first bottle was produced on Veterans Day 11-11-11, we didn't actually enter the market until 2012. I did a lot of research!

One of my favorite quotes is, "Those who don't know history are doomed to repeat it," by Edmund Burke. I knew the importance of gathering intel from my military career, and VICTORY helped to channel my intel efforts. Luckily, I don't have a fear of calling people, and I talked to anyone who I thought was an expert in distilling, vodka, and liquor distribution. I studied everyone I could think of in this industry to see how they built their business and what motivated them.

I also knew what I didn't know—the business side and accounting things, for example—and that I needed a business partner. The local small business development center introduced me to Lipman Brothers, the oldest and largest distributor of wine and spirits in Tennessee. When I called for an appointment, he said, "Look I have 100 vodkas we already carry; I'll give you 20 minutes."

Then I researched him and his company, so I knew exactly who I was talking to. I got a new suit and went down there with my PowerPoint presentation and my passion for this brand and our mission. I already had a prototype and a license, and I was looking for a business partner who was on board with my mission and vision. I knew my competition inside and out, and how I was different—and better. He took me on, and introduced me to suppliers and the best distiller.

And my intel gathering hasn't stopped. I constantly want honest feedback from my customers and the consumers so I can improve. I'm still seeking out industry giants, and finally last year I sat down with the founder of Tito's Vodka, the top-selling spirit brand in the U.S., and just talked. He was someone I had studied when I was starting my business, so it was especially meaningful to meet him.

Now Heroes Vodka is sold in 21 states. We've won numerous gold medals, including international competitions. I've become an author and a keynote speaker. I've appeared on Chelsea Lately and attended Inaugural Balls in Washington, D.C. And I have no idea how many hours of hard work I've put in, or how many miles I've put on my car making sales calls all over the country.

I know that Larry's mentorship and the strategies in VICTORY, combined with my clear mission, passion, and all my intel helped me expand beyond my wildest dreams.

Now, it's your turn! Share <u>your</u> *VICTORY* success story with me at success@larrybroughton.me. I'd love to hear from you!

*It's fine to celebrate success, but it is more important
to heed the lessons of failure.*
— Bill Gates

★ ACTION STEP: GATHER YOUR INTEL ★

Part 1: Now it's time to assess your current intel on your own business and industry. Spend two to three minutes in each category, writing down everything you know about the following:

- ★ Your own product/service/business
- ★ Your competition
- ★ Current economic opportunities and challenges in general, and for your product/service/business in particular
- ★ Any other key items for which you still need answers

How detailed is your data? Do you feel good about what you know? Where are the gaps in your intel, and how can you fill those gaps?

Part 2: Take five minutes to write down the names of every expert in your industry with whom you would like to spend an hour. Also make note of a few reasons why you'd like to meet with that particular person.

Once you've finished your list, prioritize it: are there any recurring topics on your list? People you'd like to speak to more than others? Develop and execute a plan to connect with, and engage, them using the tips in this chapter.

CHAPTER 3

COACHING

A mentor is someone
who allows you to see
the hope inside
yourself.

Oprah Winfrey

Entrepreneurs are often reluctant to ask for help because we're such a self-reliant bunch. We tend to believe that we "should" be able to figure everything out on our own, and then make it all happen without any outside assistance. We pick up this attitude because, it's true, we really *can* take care of many things independently.

Unfortunately, this mindset can (mis)lead us to think, "Don't ask for help, it's a sign of weakness." This, of course, couldn't be further from the truth. In this chapter, we'll see how a coach or mentor can move you further along the entrepreneur path faster—and how to find the right coach for you.

Key Challenge

Most entrepreneurs don't see the forest for the trees: they're too close to their own situation to make critical decisions with any kind of objectivity. In addition, they often lack the experience, the professional network, or other resources that make all the difference between creating enduring success and suffering eternal mediocrity.

Our chief want in life is somebody who will make us do what we can.
— *Ralph Waldo Emerson*

All Top Achievers Have Coaches to Help Them Reach the Next Level

Too many business owners buy into the myth and romance of the "Lone Wolf Entrepreneur" stylized by the popular media. Falling for this "go it alone" fable on your entrepreneurial journey puts both your short- and long-term success at risk. Following the Lone Wolf storyline also virtually guarantees you will struggle harder (and longer) *and* waste more of your time and money on the way to success (if you make it at all).

Are there occasional Lone Wolf success stories? Sure. However, any objective analysis of their arduous path to *eventual* success reveals it's strewn with decisions stemming from stubbornness and pride rather than clear strategic vision and analysis. In other words: yes, it could work ... but don't bank on it.

The majority of my own biggest failures happened as a direct result of trying to go it alone.

It's true: every world-class athlete, entertainer, and entrepreneur have coaches and mentors. Take a moment to reflect on this: how many top performers are you aware of that reached the pinnacle of success as a true Lone Wolf?

★ E-INSIGHT ★

The Myth of the Lone Wolf Entrepreneur

The Lone Wolf Entrepreneur is one of the most destructive myths you'll run into as a business owner, and you'll run into it constantly. This myth is a staple in popular media: TV shows, movies, and even some business magazines and business-related programs perpetuate the idea that most entrepreneurs achieve success of their own accord, pulling themselves up by the bootstraps without any need of help to succeed.

I can't say there aren't *any* Lone Wolf success stories out there. But take a look behind the curtain: you'll find there were team members, coaches, mentors, and advisors working behind the scenes to empower those "Lone Wolves" to beat the odds.

Lone Wolves make for great stories of rugged individualism, but the reality is if you really want to achieve sustained success by working smarter instead of harder, you need coaches and mentors to guide you along the way.

This has been demonstrated time and time again throughout my personal and business experience. To be honest, the vast majority of my own biggest failures and frustrations happened as a direct result of trying to go it alone. Conversely, most of my biggest successes map directly back to receiving direction and guidance from the wise counsel of coaches, mentors, and advisors who were further along the entrepreneurial path. Having learned this the hard way, I will never again operate my current or future ventures without engaging top business coaches and participating in peer-to-peer masterminds.

The bottom line? Don't hamstring yourself. This entrepreneurial gig is tough enough without falling for the Lone Wolf myth and trying to figure everything out on your own!

Coaches, mentors, teachers, advisors ... these critical success multipliers go by many different names. You might develop a formal mentor/mentee relationship with your coach, or maybe they're just someone you can call when you need a fresh perspective on a problem. The actual title and form of the relationship isn't really that important. The point is that you need a trusted advisor to help you reach the highest levels of success in the shortest time possible.

Super high achievers have recognized that we need coaches and mentors throughout our entire entrepreneurial careers. Call them what you will, but you'll want to make sure you're leveraging their skills, talents, and knowledge to your advantage, because there's absolutely no substitute for expert guidance.

The guest sees more in an hour than the host in a year.
— Polish Proverb

The Right Coach or Mentor Can Help Us Step Back, Take in The Bigger Picture

Seeing the big picture clearly is often very difficult for entrepreneurs. We are so close to our businesses—nose to the grindstone, working frantically to meet deadlines, crafting and winning proposals, pushing completed projects and finished products out the door—that we might not be able to accurately or objectively judge what's really transpiring. We may miss opportunities that are literally right in front of us, overlook critical systems flaws that can completely derail our progress, or simply be running on four cylinders instead of eight. The right coach or mentor can help us step back, take in the bigger picture, and *appreciate what it means*. This gives us the clear perspective necessary for sustained success.

There are a number of ways in which the right coach helps you achieve a high level of enduring success:

★ **The external view:** Your coach offers perspective you don't possess because you are too close to your business or too far down in the weeds. This external view is critical when making strategic decisions. Your coach helps you see what must be done, because, unlike you, s/he isn't emotionally invested in your venture.

★ **Challenging preconceived notions:** Because coaches have a different set of knowledge and experience, they'll challenge your beliefs, those things you just assume to be true. Too often, important decisions are made and actions taken based on an incomplete or inaccurate view of the realities of a situation. Your coaches help you see past these self-imposed blinders.

★ **Evaluating failures:** As I shared in the previous chapter, every entrepreneur will experience failures and the most important thing you can do is to *learn* from those failures. Conducting an effective After-Action Review[1] is critical, otherwise you won't internalize the lesson or be able to make timely adjustments. Your coach provides the framework and support for meaningful

---

[1] In the military we did an "After-Action Review" after every exercise and operation to go over what went right, what went wrong, and what can be improved next time.

COACH OR MENTOR?

Although often used interchangeably, there are a few key differences between a coach and a mentor.

	COACH	MENTOR
DURATION	Usually a specific duration	A longer-term, ongoing relationship
STRUCTURE	A formal relationship with meetings at regular intervals	More informal, with meetings set when the mentee seeks advice
SCOPE	Generally limited to a specific area of development	A holistic view of the mentee's work and life; more intimate
FOCUS	Work-related, specific and immediate goals	Both career and personal development
EXPERTISE	Need not have experience in the client's profession	Further along the mentee's path; "been there, done that"

© 2018 Larry Broughton

review, and keeps you focused on taking course-corrective action—moving forward rather than beating yourself up or wallowing in self-pity.

★ Truth-telling: It's really easy to fall in love with our own brilliant ideas and surround ourselves with people who tell us what we want to hear, instead of what we need to know. This is especially true as your organization grows because more and more of these people are added to your payroll! Your coach is sufficiently removed from your circle and has your permission to tell you the unvarnished truth, even (especially!) when you might not want to hear it.

★ Keeping you on track: Yes, even high achievers sometimes struggle through down cycles. If we don't recast our vision after a few wins, it's tempting to just relax and coast for a while. But, beware! I once heard Brian Tracy say, "There's just one direction to coast … and that's downhill." We're all challenged with the occasional season of low motivation. The input and inspiration of a coach or mentor could be just what you need to get back on the winning track.

★ Cheerleading: Finally, your coach is there to celebrate your successes. It's always great to get a pat on the back, especially from someone else who also enjoys a significant level of success. More importantly, your coach helps you objectively evaluate your "secret success sauce," how you achieved it, and learn how to replicate it.

There's just one direction to coast … and that's downhill.

Entrepreneurship can be a lonely endeavor, especially since well-meaning spouses, family, and friends who simply don't understand the entrepreneurial mindset can easily tear you down without even realizing it. The simple fact that your coach is a kindred spirit who intimately understands the entrepreneurial journey is hugely important when you hit the inevitable rough patch.

Plenty of entrepreneurs **_intellectually_** understand that a coach is just as important in business as teachers, professors, and advisors are to students during their years in university. Unfortunately, many stop there and don't take it past an intellectual exercise—they don't actually make a connection with the right coach or mentor. This is because, all too often, they get stuck in the "how" of it:

- ★ How will I know when it is time to hire a coach?
- ★ How will I know where to find the right coach?
- ★ How will I know if I am getting my money's worth?
- ★ How will I know when it is time to move on from a coaching relationship?

You'll learn the answers to these questions (and more) in the next section with concrete examples of the power of coaching.

I absolutely believe that people, unless coached,
never reach their maximum capabilities.
— Bob Nardelli, former CEO of Home Depot

Finding Your Ideal Coach

There is no doubt that a great coach/mentor can help you reach the highest levels of success in virtually all areas of business and life. But how do you find the coach that's right for you? First, seek out a coach who specializes in the area in which you desire to see specific growth. While I'm focused on business growth in this book, coaches and mentors are also invaluable in fueling personal, spiritual, relational, and professional growth. I personally tap my coaches to guide me in each of these areas when I'm feeling stuck, restless, or lost.

You're probably thinking, "OK, enough already! I understand I need a coach, but where do I go to find one?" This can be a major challenge, because there are literally tens of thousands of people out there who market themselves as business and/or life coaches (a recent Google search for "business coach" returned about 5.62 million results and the term "life coach" returned 6.85 million hits). There is virtually no entry barrier to becoming a coach and many will gladly coach you for as little as $100 or $200 per month.

Unfortunately, and for good reason, many self-styled "business experts" out there are barely scraping by. You could be their next car payment! Sure, they're cheap, but this is absolutely an area where you get exactly what you pay for.

One of my favorite maxims says: "You can't lead someone where you've never been." This is a major potential pitfall when engaging a coach. You may find someone who talks a good game, has a slick website, or promises fabulous riches and success if you become a client or buy their system. They may look perfect on the surface, but when you pull back the curtain and look a bit more carefully, their track record just doesn't match the hype.

The right coach is like a super-strength bottle of Windex®. Sometimes, being in business feels like barreling down a narrow highway at 90 miles per hour with a fogged-up, dirty windshield and a 1,000-foot drop off on each side of the road. One false move, and you're headed for disaster!

A good coach helps you wipe away the grime to gain crystal clarity. They help you zero in on specific targets, internalize lessons from your successes and failures, and map out the most direct route to your objective.

> ## A good coach is like a super-strength bottle of Windex®.

You'll want a coach who will challenge you to step up, break through the visible and invisible barriers keeping you stuck, and help you push powerfully through to the next level. Top business coaches and mentors have vast reservoirs of experience, knowledge, and connections. They're walking toolboxes filled with strategies to support you in making the leap from where you are to where you want to be. These coaches have expansive networks and will leverage those networks to connect you with other key experts, potential clients/customers, and strategic partners. This type of coach is incredibly valuable and should be viewed as an investment, not an expense.

Engaging top business coaches takes commitment and the willingness to invest in your most valuable business asset in the process—YOU! Rates vary widely

★ E-INSIGHT ★

Finding the Right Coach

How do you find a coach to help you get to the next level? Where do you start? Word of mouth, specific knowledge of your industry/clients/customers, and a proven record of success are all key markers to seek. Chances are you already know someone who is currently engaging a coach (or has in the recent past). Start by asking for recommendations from colleagues you know and trust.

Once you obtain some recommendations, gather some intel on each coach. Check out testimonials from past clients; ask about their coaching philosophy, success metrics, and the tools they use. Do a "gut check" to see if the coach seems like a good fit. In most cases, you want someone who has "been there and done that"—someone who has walked the path you're on now and is at least a bit further ahead on his/her entrepreneurial journey. While your coach doesn't necessarily need to be an expert in your specific industry, they should have proven, demonstrable success in working with business owners just like you.

As discussed in **Intel** (Chapter 2), don't discount creating a more informal mentor relationship with someone you respect who meets the criteria for a good coach. Just remember to approach them with an attitude of service so you're also offering something of value while you learn from them.

depending on the type of engagement, method of coaching delivery, how much direct access you have to the coach (as opposed to their team members), and what you are trying to accomplish in the coaching relationship. Typical investment levels include:

★ $50-$100 per month for informational programs with little direct access to the top coach

★ $500-$2,000 per month for more direct hands-on coaching with regular calls

★ $10,000 a day (or more) for a 1-on-1 in-person strategy day with the coach

You may be thinking, "There's no way in hell I would pay that much for a coach!" I get it. I've been there before and thought exactly the same thing. But ask yourself: "how expensive is it to be stuck in neutral, unable to grow your business, connect with the right clients, or hire the right staff?" A good coach can easily return five, ten, or even twentyfold your investment in them. I've experienced explosive growth in multiple businesses as a direct result of engaging the right coach.

Let's close out this section with several final thoughts on coaches and coaching relationships:

You will have a number of coaches as you advance through your entrepreneurial career. Smart business owners engage coaches to help them achieve a higher level of success and to overcome specific challenges or obstacles that are keeping them stuck. Once you've grown past the point where your current coach can assist you, it may be time to move on to another.

Chances are you will make a mistake and hire the wrong coach one day. As I said earlier, failure is part of being an entrepreneur. So, don't let hiring a bad coach sour you on coaching. Learn from your experience. I have made *major* mistakes investing in coaches and coaching programs—it happens! However, the lessons I ultimately learned from those mistakes are priceless.

Caution! Never work with a coach who is not an active participant in a coaching or mentoring program. The moment someone thinks they "know it all," you should start moving far, far away from them. I don't work with coaches or mentors who aren't continually learning and expanding their own knowledge base and network, and *neither should you*.

Ready to discover the top entrepreneurs' "Secret Weapon"—an incredibly powerful business and wealth multiplier? You'll learn all about it in the next section.

Advice after the mischief is like medicine after death.
— Danish Proverb

Mastermind Groups Are Solid Success Foundations

For some readers, the term "Mastermind Group" may be new. Or maybe you've heard the phrase, but you're not entirely clear on its meaning. Simply put, a mastermind group is a group of peers who come together on a regular schedule (be it annually, quarterly, monthly, or weekly) to mutually support each other's businesses, jointly solve tough entrepreneurial challenges, share marketing and growth ideas, and even connect fellow members with new business opportunities.

★ E-INSIGHT ★

Anatomy of a Successful Mastermind Group

I've found that all great mastermind groups share four common qualities:

★ Financial commitment. Most good mastermind groups require that members pay a fee to become part of the group. This ensures that each participant is truly committed to devoting his or her full attention to the time the group spends together.

★ Structure. The group must have a pre-defined plan for meetings, including someone to facilitate and moderate the discussions. Otherwise, the meetings can devolve into chaos with ideas flowing like water but with very little actually being accomplished.

★ Confidentiality. Each member of the group must sign and adhere to a written confidentiality agreement. This is absolutely non-negotiable; all group discussions must be kept between the group's members.

★ Accountability. Group members need to be accountable for several things, among them preparing to speak at each meeting, and being ready to offer advice and counsel to other members. Each group member should also be expected to take action on the issues they discuss with the group. Group meetings aren't gripe-fests; group members participate to gain clarity so they can take positive, forward action.

Steer clear of groups that cut corners in any of these areas.

Every mastermind group is different. Some are very informal roundtables, a group of peers who rotate the leadership position within the group, and everyone takes turns talking. Other mastermind groups are much more structured, with established leadership and rules. Some meet only by phone, others only in person, although most use a combination of the two. Still others are organized and led by an experienced coach and mentor, and are part of a larger coaching program.

Smart entrepreneurs invest heavily to participate in the right mastermind group. Most good masterminds require a financial commitment of $7,500 to $25,000 annually and top entrepreneurs routinely invest $250,000 (or more) to participate in very high-level groups. Before you throw this book down in disgust and call these folks a bunch of fools, try to wrap your head around the lifetime value of a single major business breakthrough or great idea. I've personally witnessed the creation of multimillion dollar ideas in mastermind groups. It's actually quite common, and it's *always* exciting!

Most top groups are highly structured and participants are serious both about their own business and about helping others succeed. You get the opportunity to present your biggest business challenge, opportunity, or idea before the group, and after your presentation, other group members ask clarifying questions. Then you move on to a group brainstorming session; these sessions are always dynamic and can be very unpredictable!

I've personally witnessed the creation of multimillion dollar ideas in mastermind groups.

Members often come up with completely novel ways for you to get something done, vastly improve on your existing idea or even let you know if it just isn't worth pursuing. The room is often filled with electric energy as members problem-solve and explore possibilities from a dozen different angles. The power of having eight to 12 brilliant entrepreneurial minds focused on *your* business idea (or challenge) is incredible.

This is the true genius of the mastermind format.

One of the reasons that mastermind groups can be so effective is that people pay good money to be part of the group. They're invested, literally and figuratively. That means two things: first, it means *people come prepared*. They're ready to discuss the problems that keep their businesses from moving forward. Before the group comes together, everyone has thought through what they're going to say; they've done their homework. This ensures that time spent with the group is productive for everyone involved.

Second, the fact that people pay to be part of the group means that they come ready to **help other people**. There is an expectation that everyone in the group will help each other, and people give their honest attention to what others are saying. There's a real spirit of cooperation, and a desire to make sure everyone in the group succeeds—meaning, you get the best from everyone. One aspect of mastermind groups that makes them so dynamic is that they consist of people from different backgrounds, with different areas of expertise. One member may own a public relations business, while another runs a security firm, another is a CPA, and yet another is an independent martial arts instructor. With that much variety in the room, you **know** your problems will be examined from many different angles.

An effective mastermind group also holds you accountable to take action on the things that are preventing you from moving forward. Once you've brought up an issue for group discussion, you can't come to the next meeting without having taken action. It's a great source of motivation for those who tend to put off facing problems.

There are two main concerns that sometimes keep people away from mastermind groups. The first concern is about confidentiality. After all, you're sharing problems and ideas with a room full of people. Couldn't one of them steal your idea of a product or service, implement it, and make an easy fortune with your idea?

In reality, this simply doesn't happen. First of all, good mastermind groups (remember, you get what you pay for) consist of people who are there to serve and contribute, not to steal your thunder. To ensure the safety of everyone's intellectual property, each group member must sign a Confidentiality, Non-Disclosure and Non-Circumvent Agreement, ensuring issues discussed within the group stay there.

The second concern many people share is about others soliciting their services within the group. After all, if you've got a PR guy and a copywriter in your group, what's to keep them from using the mastermind meeting to drum up new business for themselves?

In a *good* mastermind group, this rarely happens. People are there to give and receive feedback, not to self-promote. Mastermind meetings are not networking events, where you hand out business cards and try to sign up new

---

★ E-INSIGHT ★

It's Lonely at the Top

I've spoken with many people who are leaders of large organizations. One thing that rings true for many of them is that being at the top of a company can be extremely lonely. It's not practical for them to go to their subordinates to kick around some of their more potent ideas, and they may not have a management team in place they can depend on to explore different business options. So, they are left to make decisions on their own.

This is where a coach or mastermind group can be extremely helpful. This is where such a leader can get honest feedback, share sensitive business ideas in a safe environment, and even get their butt kicked when necessary. A coaching and/or mastermind arrangement provides a safe place for senior leaders to give and receive solid, objective business advice.

---

clients. Most groups I'm familiar with actually police themselves—if someone is there to promote their own business, other members of the group can and do request they either stop or leave.

I often leave my mastermind group meetings with page after page of innovative ideas. We learn from people analyzing our own problems, as well as from participating in group discussions about the problems others are facing. Mastermind groups are a unique mix of advisory panel, support group, accountability partners, and cheerleading squad!

It's no coincidence that many of the successful entrepreneurs I know are part of mastermind groups. Mastermind sessions will stretch your brain, allow you to think about things in different ways, bring new approaches to light, and encourage you to manage the problems you're facing *now*. If you're not part of a mastermind group, you're missing out—take advantage of this "secret weapon" for entrepreneurial success!

★ VICTORY SUCCESS STORY ★

Before I met Larry, I had been part of a coaching franchise. It was my first foray into coaching and, in a way, it was the perfect setup. The company had all the materials and strategies, so I didn't have to reinvent the wheel. But the company didn't last.

I had to repurpose what I'd done and build a coaching practice on my own. But the bigger issue for me was how to replace the sense of community I had with this company. It's hard going from

Steve Smith
Business & Executive Coach
GrowthSource Coaching

an environment where you have comrades and people around you to being a party of one. I was having trouble keeping my head in the game (and I'm a coach, remember. How ironic is that?).

I knew I needed to replicate the community of support I'd had with the franchise. That's what Larry and his mastermind group provided for me. It helped rebuild the support and colleague-type relationships most small businesses lack. Larry's mentorship really helped me rebuild my confidence. Turns out, even coaches need a coach!

To me, there are two reasons to get a coach. The first is pace—being held accountable for your goals and gathering momentum to go faster than you can on your own. The second—and this is where Larry's mentorship made such a difference for me—is scope. We tend to think too small, not that we mean to. It just happens. A coach opens up your ability to see things on a much bigger scale. Business can be hard if you don't get ahead of it, and Larry helped me broaden my thinking.

A real point of clarity came when I joined a business networking group in Orange County, California where I live. At the end of my first meeting, a gentleman I knew came up to me and said, "You do realize that in this group, coaching has no currency. People don't believe coaching is a real profession." I thought that perhaps they didn't value business coaching because they had probably never met a good one.

There and then I set my intention to be the most authentic business coach this group, filled with lawyers and money managers, had ever seen. I would show them what I do, how I do it, and who benefits from it—and show them measurable success and return on investment. I'm happy to say that I've gotten several clients from the group, and most people in the group now recognize and value what I do as a business coach.

Now, it's your turn! Share <u>your</u> *VICTORY* success story with me at success@larrybroughton.me. I'd love to hear from you!

I feel really grateful to the people who encouraged me and helped me develop. Nobody can succeed on their own.
— *Sheryl Sandberg, Chief Operating Officer of Facebook*

★ ACTION STEP: GET A COACH ★

Part 1: Think about a personal or professional experience where you connected with the right coach or mentor. What challenge did that connection help you overcome? What was the value to you personally and professionally?

Now connect with the present day. What major obstacle or challenge are you currently facing in your business? Is a portion of your start-up plan driving you crazy? What other area of your life would improve if you connected with someone who could help you work through it from a place of experience and knowledge?

Homework assignment: find yourself a coach to help you tackle your biggest frustration by this time <u>next</u> week!

Part 2: Perform an honest self-assessment of your skills, resources, talents, and experiences. What could you bring to the table in a mastermind group that would be valuable to the other members? Keep in mind that the success of the group depends on its members being prepared to give generously.

Remember not to discount any of your skills or talents just because they're easy for you. We often fail to value that which comes effortlessly to us. Something you find simple may be exceedingly difficult for others to master— we're all different! Focusing on these areas is a great way to contribute lasting value to the group.

_____

_____

_____

_____

_____

_____

_____

_____

_____

_____

_____

_____

_____

_____

_____

_____

_____

_____

_____

CHAPTER 4

TEAM BUILDING

Alone we can do so little, together we can do so much.

Helen Keller

Some of the most significant challenges in life can be overcome more easily with good ol' teamwork. After all, teamwork makes facing life's challenges a whole lot more fun!

The truth is, we are born to interact with others … at first with family and then through life with friends, colleagues, and community. In fact, the most enjoyment in achieving anything worthwhile in life is in sharing it with others.

Likewise, the most successful entrepreneurs have a great team around them. In this chapter, I'll redefine what a team could mean for your business and how to hire the right people.

Key Challenge

As I shared in the previous chapter, too many entrepreneurs buy into the Lone Wolf myth of successful entrepreneurship. They try to do too many things themselves, without attempting to build an effective team. No organization can exist for long, let alone create enduring success, without assembling a highly effective team.

Many aspiring entrepreneurs break into a cold sweat at the first mention of "building a team," as visions of payroll taxes and micro-management nightmares dance through their heads. But the truth is much more palatable: teams can now take many forms, from 100 percent virtual workforces who are contracted as independent providers to the traditional multi-location organization structure with hundreds, thousands, or even tens of thousands of W-2 team members. The principles of team-building you'll learn in this chapter are applicable to every business, regardless of size or complexity.

If everyone is moving forward together,
then success takes care of itself.
— Henry Ford

A Great Team Is Essential to Everyone's Success

Consider what you learned about **Coaching** in Chapter 3. Hopefully, you surely recognize that the Lone Wolf approach to entrepreneurial success is ***not*** one you should embrace, as it significantly limits your ability to effectively start and grow your business on virtually every front. Understanding this point is crucial when building a winning organization. To put it bluntly, you will never create the business you envision, the life you desire, or the positive impact you are capable of creating without putting the right team in place.

In fact, huge leaps in technology and connectivity now let you craft a globally-based team of extraordinary talent with incredible ease. You can farm out specific tasks to people who do amazing work for a *fraction* of the cost of a traditional full-time employee. Obviously, that's tremendously beneficial for entrepreneurs in startup mode when capital is usually very tight.

Also note that I jettison the term "employee" in favor of "team member." I firmly believe that the latter is far more positive and better reflects rapidly changing business dynamics. Being a *team member* is all about shared vision and empowerment. It's a far cry from the old-school servant vs. overseer relationships that many companies seem to be built on.

Be cautious about fixating on preconceived ideas about what your team "*should*" look like, especially those stemming from conventional wisdom. If there's one thing you can count on, it's change, so your most important initial step is building a team that can successfully support your mission-critical tasks for the next one to two years. Don't lock yourself into a long-term team structure.

The most important element in building a good team is actually knowing yourself.

Your needs will likely change significantly as your business grows, the marketplace shifts and new technologies emerge. Focus on your vision for future success, but allow for substantial flexibility around your team as you look ahead five, ten, 15 years, and beyond.

Without question, the most important (and unfortunately, most frequently overlooked) element in building a good team is actually knowing your*self*. I'll explore this in detail a bit later, but for now remember to avoid the common mistake of hiring people who are just like you. Instead, hire people whose abilities and personalities **complement** your own, who cover gaps in your knowledge or experience, strengthen your weak points, and most importantly, allow you to focus on doing what you do best.

The *Kolbe A Index* and the *CliftonStrengths* assessments I recommend are both great tools to help you more fully connect with your inherent strengths and passions. They give you an objective picture of your inherent strengths, actionable information on how you should spend your time, and how best to approach various tasks.

If you haven't done so yet, please, right now, go take the _CliftonStrengths_ and _Kolbe A Index_ assessments. The insights you'll gain are invaluable guides as you begin to assemble your team.

Let's face it: most of us find it hard to admit we aren't great at everything. From kindergarten on, we're taught to spend excessive amounts of time and effort trying to fix our **perceived** weaknesses instead of focusing on our **real** strengths. But guess what? The truth is you're **not** great at everything, and heck, you might not even be great at most things!

Albert Einstein once said: *"Everybody is a genius. But if you judge a fish by its ability to climb a tree, it will live its whole life believing that it is stupid."*

You possess a unique combination of three to five core abilities—areas in which where you are simply brilliant. These are your strengths. Focus on them with laser-like intensity and leverage them to your advantage. Delete, delegate, or defer everything else to your custom-built team.

On a related note, this is a good time to review your notes from **Vision** (Chapter 1). To effectively build a team that buys into your vision, it *must* be clear in your own mind. If you don't have crystal clarity around your vision, how will you be able to convey it to your team members?

There are three common misconceptions that prevent entrepreneurs from starting or expanding their teams, even when they already *know* they need to do so. These are:

★ **"It takes too long to train someone.":** While it's true that training team members does take time, if you clearly identify your vision and values, and hire people who align with them, your training investment creates team members who magnify the strength and effectiveness of your organization.

★ **"It's quicker and easier to do things yourself.":** When you first hire someone, you probably can do their job more quickly than they can. You can also probably do it better than they can. So, what do you need them for? Ask yourself this: Are you doing the things at which you excel, those things that will result in long-term success for your business? Or are you too busy doing the things others should be doing, the things in which *they* excel? Your team members will increase their speed and efficiency as they gain experience, provided you hire the right people – and leverage their strengths appropriately.

★ **"It's too expensive to hire a team.":** Doing everything yourself is a waste of your time and energy, because you spend time doing things that don't build your business. You're significantly limiting your own success! Your team expands your ability to focus on what you're best at, freeing you up to succeed. Look at it this way: it's actually too expensive **not** to hire a team. Makes a lot of sense, doesn't it?

The last misconception gets right to the heart of the problem. Too many entrepreneurs consider hiring team members (or coaches, or anything else that doesn't directly put dollars into their bank accounts) as an expense. In reality, they are ***investments in the future success of your business***. Surrounding yourself with the right people exponentially expands your opportunities to build long-term success. Resources invested in training and developing your team members invariably results in a stronger, more effective organization.

You might be thinking, "this all sounds well and good, but I'm already tight on cash **and** time. How the heck do I budget for this?" Good question! I'll dive deep into the answers in the next section.

Individual commitment to a group effort—that is what makes a team work, a company work, a society work, a civilization work.
— Vince Lombardi, NFL Coach

How to Build a Team That Ensures Long-Term Success

A group could be any set of people who have something in common— attending a summit, or working in a certain field, for example. But it takes much more than warm bodies to make a *team*. A team is a group of people who also subscribe to a common mission. Each member of a team works with, and supports, the others for a greater good; a shared vision or goal. That's why your biggest task in team-building is to effectively communicate your own vision and values to your team members.

You need to communicate the vision and values of your company early on in the hiring process. You must be clear, open, and honest about what's important in your organization. When you clearly outline your values and vision from the very beginning of the hiring process, it becomes much easier to attract the right people (and weed out the wrong ones). People who buy into your vision will be much more motivated to accomplish great things, both for your organization and for themselves.

It is imperative to focus your team building efforts towards those who share your vision, values, and other key traits. I believe far too many entrepreneurs overemphasize the importance of skills and experience when hiring. People can always learn new skills and gain more experience, but it is extremely difficult to *train* certain qualities into someone … they either have "it" or they don't.

There are three traits that simply cannot be taught (trust me here; it's a wasted and time-consuming effort), and each of your potential team members must exhibit them all. These traits are *motivation*, *integrity,* and the *capacity to grow*.

Your team members must be motivated: they need to "bring it" every day on

---

★ **E-INSIGHT** ★

Motivation, Integrity, and the Capacity to Grow

Too many entrepreneurs hire team members based solely on the new hire's experience, knowledge, or skill set. This can often be a mistake, because while you can teach people knowledge and skills you cannot teach integrity and core values. Thus, integrity and core values should be the first things you look for when hiring someone new.

A new team member who buys into your organization's vision, and possesses integrity, is a strong asset for your company even if you'll need to fill in some gaps in their knowledge or skill set. Look for these innate qualities in every person you hire.

---

every project. However, motivation without integrity is dangerous. You could end up with someone who genuinely wants to get things done and achieve, but is willing to cut corners and act against your core values to accomplish their goals. In addition, if you hire people who possess both motivation and integrity, but lack the capacity to grow, they will eventually slow—or potentially even *stop*—the forward progress of your organization.

Ideally, you're looking for someone who possesses all three character traits, shares your values, and who already has the experience and skills you need. But if you find someone who's motivated, has integrity, can grow with your company, and who shares your values, *hire them immediately*, even if they don't have all the experience you want. Remember: skills and knowledge can be taught; critical traits and core values cannot.

One reason it's so important to hire people with these qualities is it only takes one bad team member to disrupt and poison an otherwise effective team. A person who lacks integrity will cost you customers and, ultimately, your reputation, while an unmotivated team member is dead weight that will hold your organization back and adversely affect the morale of others.

Slow to hire, quick to fire.

It's always difficult to fire a team member, especially when that person is successful or possesses a skill that is uncommon or difficult to acquire. Nobody likes bringing down the axe, and many business owners, especially in the early stages, simply turn a blind eye to the shortcomings of someone who is bringing revenue into their companies. My own experience is that it's better to fire people quickly, before they have the chance to wreck the morale and effectiveness of the rest of the team than to allow problems to incubate. My mantra is "slow to hire, quick to fire."

That's not to say you should go out and start firing people for arbitrary reasons, but when you see someone really isn't an ideal fit, it's usually best to sever the relationship as soon as possible. If you have current team members, most of them probably work on an at-will basis, meaning you can let them go at any time. Of course, always make sure you document all of your conversations, as well as the different ways you tried to bring the worker's performance up to speed. The bottom line is when someone is a poor fit for your company in the beginning, they will still be a poor fit a year, five years, or ten years down the line. I know it can be challenging, but it's best to fire them quickly. At the end of this section, I'll share a story from my personal experience about letting a new hire go rather quickly.

You should protect yourself by having a written set of standard procedures in place that fully outlines your process for hiring, working with, and firing team members. You'll learn more about developing effective Standard Operating Procedures ("SOP") in **Operations** (Chapter 5).

I strongly recommend you to evaluate all new hires for your team through a 90-day probationary or introductory period, during which you retain the option of letting them go for virtually any reason. This three-month "test drive" will enable you to answer some important questions:

- ★ Does your new hire really understand your vision and values?
- ★ Are they self-motivated to produce results?
- ★ Do they display the integrity you demand from your team?
- ★ Are they quick learners who will continuously grow with your company?

Chances are you'll get all the answers you need within the first two weeks of the introductory period. It's much like dating: you can usually tell after a date or two whether you're compatible—you just "click." All too often, entrepreneurs hold out until day 88 or 89 of the probationary period in forlorn hope that their poorly-suited hire will miraculously turn around.

If your new hire isn't working out, be open and honest about it, and then set them free as early as possible. Otherwise, you're wasting your own valuable time and energy along with theirs. Don't let the *right* person for your team slip away because you were too busy trying to "fix" someone who was never a good fit in the first place.

I've put this concept into practice. Years ago, I was a partner in a fast-growth company and we found it was time to stop outsourcing our monthly accounting and financial statement preparation, and bring it in-house. It was clear that not having a senior financial executive in the organization was holding us back from our potential and our growth goals. This was a big step for us, as it was the added burden of a senior executive salary, but we realized that having a Chief Financial Officer on board, with more experience than we had, was going to be a key driver to our success in producing timely and accurate financial statements and raising capital.

After an exhaustive search, conducting several impressive interviews and checking references, we hired a very experienced CFO. We were excited about bringing this person onboard and even a little surprised that they had accepted the position, based on their pedigree and experience, and the fact that their starting salary with us was significantly lower than their past positions We chalked it up to buying into our vision and the possibility of growing with us.

We made the announcement to our leadership team and managers, and could hardly wait for the start date. Prior to the CFO's official start date, we met and reinforced our core values, discussed our corporate culture, and set some short-, mid-, and long-term goals for the CFO and the new department.

It wasn't 48-hours after the start date that we began getting comments and calls from our team members asking who the heck had we hired. As it turns out, our new CFO was very disrespectful to other managers, was condescending, and made disparaging comments about the state of our financials and accounting functions. One manager mentioned that our new CFO made the comment, *"What have I gotten myself into? I shouldn't have taken this job."* I assure you, we were very clear about the state of our accounting (or lack of accounting) department. Rather than speak to the opportunity and show excitement about being on the team, this person focused on the negative.

As soon as we heard this news, we spoke with the CFO, asked tons of questions, and restated some of our core values, which included: direct and respectful communication at all times, positive and upbeat attitudes, and a can-do spirit. The CFO said the right things, apologized, and talked about being simply overwhelmed with the amount of work that needed to be done. We ended the meeting on a positive note.

Within 24-hours, we were receiving frantic calls and complaints from managers who said the CFO had called them in a tirade—after our meeting where we discussed our core values—letting them know that their lives would be miserable because they spoke up about the CFO's disrespectful tone. Making retaliatory calls was (and still is) the antithesis of our values and vision for the organization. Do you see the irony in the CFO's actions? I'll wrap this up by saying we immediately separated this CFO's employment with us, and I reflected on where we went wrong.

The truth was, we made that hire based more on experience than on core values, motivation, or integrity. When we made the announcement to our team that the CFO was no longer with us, the dark cloud that had hung over the organization for the past few days had cleared and key team members gave a sigh of relief.

We made that hire based more on experience than on core values, motivation, or integrity.

Leaders throughout the organization later commented that they appreciated that we held true to our company core values and were willing to protect the organization's commitment to a positive culture. The unexpected side effects of this event led to increased loyalty of our rock star performers, increased engagement, and more attention to the details of accounting and financial services. We didn't replace the CFO immediately, but we did ultimately hire one who served us well by acting a lot more like a mentor than a tyrant.

I hope this real-life example gives you some insight and some courage the next time you have to make a difficult decision to let a team member go.

In the next section, I'll help you figure out exactly who you want on your team and how to forge those people into a strong, sharp, and capable organization.

The strength of the team is each individual member.
The strength of each member is the team.
— Phil Jackson, NBA Coach

Building Your Team for Peak Performance (and Keeping It There)

Many entrepreneurs share a common weakness: we tend to hire people who are just like us. I call this the "Mini-Me Syndrome" (with apologies to Mike

Myers). I've fallen into this trap when building both traditional and virtual teams and it's completely understandable.

There's a degree of comfort and familiarity involved when you hire people who have a similar background to your own. Parallel skill sets, shared experiences and similar world views feed this comfort level. You tend to look at things the same way, use the same problem-solving approaches and even come to the exact same solutions. Sounds great, right? My answer is an emphatic "NO!" This is usually a *terrible* way to build an effective team.

If you succumb to Mini-Me Syndrome, your team will let many critical functions fall through the cracks. Why? Because if your team shares all of your personal strengths, they probably also share many of the same weaknesses and blind spots. Everyone will avoid the weak spots, leaving these important tasks to pile up until they become overwhelming!

Instead, hire strategically. Hire people who complement your strengths and interests; find people who excel doing tasks that you do not, but that they love doing. They'll help you pick up the slack in the areas where you're weakest. This is why self-knowledge—awareness of your inherent strengths and passions—is essential, and why I stress the importance of the assessments I mentioned in the Introduction and in the first section of this chapter. Without this knowledge, it's hard to even know where to begin building your team, but once you've acquired it, you're able to act quickly to fill the gaps.

So far, this chapter has focused on forming *new* teams. What if you already have a team of people around you? The exact same principles apply. Once we've communicated our vision for growth, expansion, improved standards, and increased expectations, it's critical we reassess whether our current team members have the capacity to contribute or keep up with our plan.

Start by having each key team member take the _Kolbe A Index_ and _CliftonStrengths_ assessments. I recommend using a certified Kolbe Consultant to analyze the Kolbe results, especially if your team is very large. These results will provide invaluable insight into your team's strong points, as well as where adjustments, realignment, or new hires are necessary.

One common finding after reviewing these assessments is that some existing team members aren't a great fit for their current positions. You may need to realign their responsibilities, move them to a different position, or place them within a different internal team. If they can't (or won't) make these adjustments to better align your team, it's time for them to go. I like to say, "coach 'em up, or coach 'em out."

Assuming we've surrounded ourselves with people who are highly motivated and possess a boatload of integrity, the lack of capacity to grow (and change) with us may be the one thing that drives people out the door. As leaders, we have a duty to coach team members towards their fullest potential (more on that in the next section); if, however, they simply lack the ability to keep up, we have a moral obligation to ourselves, and our high-performing team members, to coach them out of the organization. By coaching them out, I mean we must (in a humane, supportive, dignified, and respectful manner) set them free to find work and excel in a place that's a better fit for them.

It's always painful to let people go, especially if they've been with you for a while. But sometimes it's the only way to position your organization to peak

---

★ E-INSIGHT ★

Just Because I Can...

Just because you *can* do something doesn't mean you *should* do it. The "Pareto Principle" states that 80 percent of your results in business (and in life) stem from just 20 percent of your activity. For example, most companies find that around 80 percent of their revenues come from 20 percent of their customers and clients, and that 20 percent of their sales staff generates about 80 percent of the company's sales.

How does this apply to you? You must concentrate your efforts on a small set of activities that deliver the greatest benefits. Most entrepreneurs try to do far too many things in their organizations, spreading themselves too thin and getting bogged down with trivial tasks for which they are ill-suited. The result? They don't have enough remaining bandwidth to focus on the true essentials.

The Action Step at the end of this chapter will help you identify your "Top 20" or so activities. Focus as much time and energy on them as possible. Delegate, outsource, or delete everything else! Don't be the choke point in your own business.

---

performance. As always, make sure you follow your SOP and document all interactions with team members.

Your ultimate goal in building and/or adjusting your team is to free yourself to do the things you do well; the things you are passionate about … the things that make money. For the majority of entrepreneurs, these are also the critical, revenue-generating tasks most profitable to their businesses. Focus on the three to five areas where you shine, such as making the sales pitch, managing client relationships, networking with key decision makers, creating unique content, or providing strategic direction for the rest of the team.

You are the Maestro, and it's your job as the leader of your organization to conduct the orchestra (your team) for maximum effectiveness. Make it a priority to delegate or outsource anything you don't do well (or really dislike doing); focus on your key role and empower your team to take care of everything else.

You are the Maestro. It's your job to conduct the orchestra for maximum effectiveness!

Of course, none of this happens with the wave of a magic wand. It will take some time to hire the right people and make the necessary adjustments to get your team firing on all cylinders. In the next section, I'm going to share some of the most successful tools I've found to create happy and productive teams.

TEAM BUILDING 1-2-3

1
INSPIRE

Communicate an aspirational vision, and each team member's role in achieving it. Inspire them towards success and benchmark their accomplishments and contributions.

HOW

Listen to the team's needs. Identify their values. Learn what makes them tick. Share information freely. Become a master storyteller to paint pictures of shared success.

2
ACTIVATE

Activate their energy. Lead by example and demonstrate what success looks like. Motivate, demonstrate, and invest in professional development.

HOW

Invest time and money in strengths-based performance. Delegate outcomes, not tasks; create an action-oriented, results-driven climate. Demonstrate, instruct, and offer feedback.

3
CHEER/CHALLENGE

Become your team members' biggest cheerleader, champion and challenger. Remain positive, but do not accept mediocrity.

HOW

Continually challenge towards excellence and affirm their worth and value to the team. Tolerate mistakes and learn from them. Recognize, articulate, and believe in their potential. Celebrate successes often.

A good attitude won't guarantee victory,
but a bad one will guarantee defeat.
— *Larry Broughton*

Creating the Environment to Sustain Your Elite Team

We're delusional if we think we can simply gather a group of high achievers and expect them to perform as a team with enduring growth and success. But with some time, dedication, and occasionally some tough decisions, you will create an inspired, productive, and happy team that is aligned with your vision. And then, my friend, greatness is within reach.

It's important to assess the culture of your organization and create an environment in which your rockstar team members will thrive. To paraphrase Richard Branson, if you take care of your team members, they'll take care of your customers.

We all want to be happy at work, right? After all, most of us will spend at least a third (if not more) of our waking hours at work. Promoting happiness at work includes creating a work environment where team members are valued, cheered on towards success, challenged, and stretched; where all members understand and work towards a common vision; and where they are professionally developed and working in their strengths.

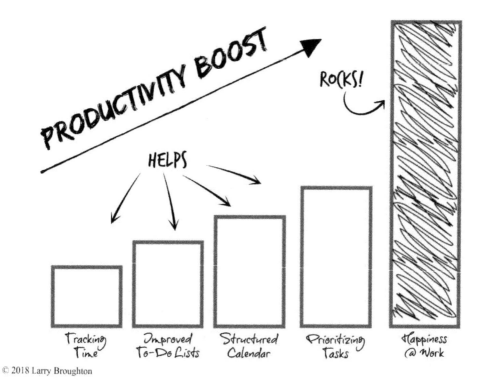

These elements cultivate a happy work environment and leads to a greater boost in productivity than any time-tracking tool, new-fangled to-do list, shared calendar apps, or prioritization of tasks.

Achieving "happiness at work" also means investing time and attention in your team members. Here are my top five tips to minimize internal strife and conflict within an organization:

★ **Listen to Team Members.** Take the time to gather feedback from your team members to determine how they feel about their jobs, roles, and responsibilities. You can do this through informal chats, confidential work climate surveys, formal information gathering meetings, etc. To solicit quality feedback, keep meetings nonthreatening, and encourage team members to speak freely. Whenever possible, implement changes they suggest to show you value their opinions and to encourage future dialogue.

★ **Discover Their Goals.** A significant part of the listening process involves asking team members about their long-term goals and ambitions. This not only demonstrates you're interested in the professional development of your team, but gives you the opportunity to uncover some hidden talent or skill that could benefit the organization. Help team members develop an action plan to reach their goals.

★ **Praise Good Work Publicly.** Catch them doing something right! During a busy workday, it's easy to overlook the accomplishments of the team members and mention only their mistakes. An occasional handwritten note acknowledging achievements to let them know you appreciate their daily effort goes a long way toward providing motivation and building morale.

★ **Make Corrections Quickly and Privately.** If you notice a team member doing something incorrectly or behaving in an unacceptable manner, don't let the situation escalate. Without delay, talk to the team member in private. View this as an opportunity to teach instead of to reprimand. If you wait until you become angry over repeated occurrences, you're more likely to become confrontational in your approach, which can alienate you from the team member.

★ **Set an Example.** Show team members how they should go about their work by setting an example. If you expect teammates to follow through on promises to customers, set a positive example by fulfilling your promises. If you spend a lot of time gossiping at the water cooler and badmouthing clients, you send the message that it's acceptable for them to do the same.

Another great assessment for your organization is where you fall on what I call the "Productivity-Positivity Matrix." Be brave, take a look at the matrix on the next page, and assess where you are.

Those organizations low in both productivity *and* positivity are standing at death's door and will soon expire. A total corporate overhaul is needed to survive (or a reservation made at the corporate morgue). Those who are high in productivity, yet low in positivity, are likely grinding out an existence and burning through their human capital—these organizations are in need of soothing relief in the form of team member recognition; improved work conditions; effective incentive programs; up-beat, humane leadership; and perhaps some team member autonomy.

Organizations with low productivity, yet high positivity, may have laid the groundwork by developing an upbeat, light-as-a-cloud work environment, but need to make a course correction soon by instituting productivity goals; performance metrics; clearly articulating expectations; and identifying team leaders to motivate, inspire, and act as role models. Left unchecked, the corporate coffin will be carried to the grave by happy, unemployed pallbearers.

Those blessed organizations with high productivity *and* positivity are destined for greatness. To maintain the spirit of success, they must loosen the corporate reins on their stallions and offer the freedom to run full bore. They must systematize and automate operations when possible and celebrate success often. More importantly, however, they must embrace and

THE PRODUCTIVITY-POSITIVITY MATRIX

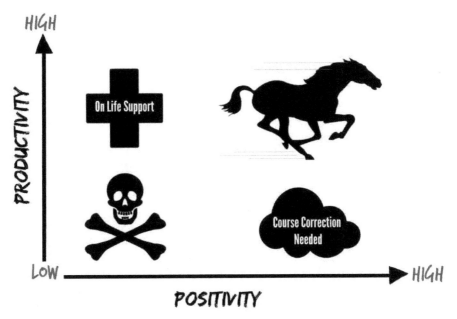

© 2018 Larry Broughton

learn from their failures. Leaders who have identified those elements of their organization's culture that have contributed to success and then ensured they are ingrained in the corporate DNA, are more likely to defy the odds and secure enduring success.

Once you do have everything humming along at peak efficiency, how do you sustain that momentum? The best way to accomplish this is to make sure the entire team stays focused on the shared vision and goals of your organization. Revisit the strategy points in Vision (Chapter 1). Keep that vision front and center and make sure your team understands it. Clearly communicate your vision to your team on a regular basis; explain where you're going and why you're going there as an organization.

When people have a clear picture of your larger vision, it's much easier for them to buy into it. Otherwise, they'll end up working on unconnected pieces of a jigsaw puzzle—without the advantage of seeing the photo on the box. Team members get frustrated when they don't see how their activities contribute to the larger picture. Strongly consider holding regular team meetings to share what's going on, recognize team members for outstanding performance and answer any questions. You can do this in person, over the phone, or with a video-conferencing application like Zoom, Skype, or Google Plus if your team is virtual or geographically dispersed.

Best of all, it doesn't need to take long—maybe 30 minutes at the most—and it really keeps people engaged. Lay out the key goals for the week and big events coming up in the near future. And don't be afraid to table a vexing challenge and ask for solutions!

As your team grows, it's also a good idea to consider one or more strategic retreats each year so you can take a step back from the day-to-day operations of the business and evaluate the challenges, obstacles, and opportunities your organization is facing. I strongly recommend using outside facilitators for strategic retreats for a variety of reasons, including objectivity, full engagement by all team members, and having an external observer to keep you on track.

Finally, when you hire good people, allow them some freedom to maneuver. Give them the mission parameters: the goal, the timeline for completion, and any key touch points along the way. Empower them with the authority and autonomy necessary to succeed … and then get out of the way! Let your team take over. Let them implement strategies to get everything done. Give them permission for a "touch and go" if they have questions or need clarification, and make sure they know you trust them to accomplish your goals.

Building a team like this to get things done for you frees you from the constant worry that slows so many entrepreneurs to a crawl. It's exciting, invigorating, and liberating because it allows you to follow your passion: to stay connected with why you became an entrepreneur in the first place!

★ VICTORY SUCCESS STORY ★

When I met Larry and read VICTORY, *my company was half the size we are now. At the time, I knew I wanted to grow the business, but I discovered there aren't a lot of tools or advice to help you grow a business. There's a lot out there to* <u>start</u> *a business, but not to grow one, and it was outside my scope as a business owner.*

Bobbie Hurley O'Dell
Co-Owner / Vice President
Arpco Valves & Controls

I didn't have a goal or a vision of what that growth would look like, but once I focused on building a great company culture and solidifying our team, we had the foundation to grow.

The vibe around the office when I first bought the company with my business partner felt like "every man for himself." There was a lot of finger-pointing and backstabbing, and people working towards their personal goals, not the company's goals.

One of the first things I did was shift from "employees" to "team members" based on Larry's advice in the book. I recently asked everyone at one of our company's leadership classes (another new team-building thing we do now) if they liked that change, and it was a unanimous "YES!" They really do feel like they're part of a team now.

Owning a company with a partner is a lot like a marriage: your spouse doesn't always listen to you, but if someone else says the same thing, they'll listen. So, a few years ago, I decided (with Larry's advice) that we needed to do a company-wide team member satisfaction survey. I wanted to see how the team perceived we were managing the company.

Well, I cried for about two days when the survey results came in. The team's perception of me was that I didn't care about the company, that I was scattered, and didn't want to talk to them because I was better than them. I was shocked, because in my mind, nothing was further from the truth—the company was my life. I felt a deep responsibility for each team member and their families. I was working hard, putting in long hours and being totally focused when I got to the office.

But they didn't see it that way, so I made a lot of changes. Now I make the rounds when I get to the office. I check in with the team to see what's happening and how things are going. My communication with our management and all of our team members has improved. It can take me 30 minutes to get to my desk, whereas before I went straight into my office to get to work.

I'm so proud of the culture we've created at our company. Our team members enjoy coming to work, and it feels like we are a family. Developing a mission statement, defining our core values, assigning responsibility, and taking action on our ideas ... all of the things I implemented because of Larry's strategies have helped to create a strong company culture. And we've grown because of it.

Now, it's your turn! Share your *VICTORY* success story with me at success@larrybroughton.me. I'd love to hear from you!

The main ingredient to stardom is the rest of the team.
— John Wooden, Legendary Basketball Coach

★ ACTION STEP: DO WHAT YOU DO BEST ★

Part 1: Take a sheet of paper, and divide it into three columns. Title the first column "Doing," the second column "Great At," and the third column "Love It." In the *Doing* column, list all of the things you are actually doing in your business at the moment. This means everything, from the smallest menial job to the most important client meeting. In the *Great At* column, list all the things you do that you are great at doing. In the *Love It* column, write down the things you do that you really enjoy doing.

Now, circle the items you listed in both the *Great At* and *Love It* columns. Those are the activities on which you need to concentrate. They are most likely the areas of your business you are best at and most passionate about.

As for the other items on your list, they are *all* wasting your time. Delegate or eliminate them and get busy accomplishing the things you do best!

Part 2: Choose one thing from your 3-Column Exercise in Part 1 that you can have a team member take over. If you don't have a team, using the tips in this chapter, write out a position profile (aka job description) and what attributes the person should possess. And then hire that person!

Part 3: If you already have a team, choose three things discussed in this chapter you can implement this quarter to create a positive and productive company culture, and write out a plan to do them.

_____

_____

_____

_____

_____

_____

_____

_____

_____

_____

_____

_____

_____

_____

_____

_____

_____

_____

_____

_____

_____

CHAPTER  5

OPERATIONS

There is nothing so useless as doing efficiently that which should not be done at all.

Peter F. Drucker

Operations are the support systems that enable your success. They are a necessary part of playing the game in today's business world. Many entrepreneurs have no systems in place, or their systems are in their heads where no one else can see them.

In this chapter, I'll dive into the purpose and benefits of operations and systems—and give you simple ways you can start creating your operations manual today.

Key Challenge

Many aspiring entrepreneurs fail to create clear, easily implemented and repeatable systems within their businesses or, if these are developed, fail to employ them consistently. Not having proper systems in place from startup forward prevents growth, lowers the value of your business to potential buyers, and can ultimately lead to the utter collapse of the organization.

If you're like most entrepreneurs, you probably find working on the functional systems of your business about as exciting as watching paint dry. You'd probably prefer to concentrate on the *fun* stuff, like interacting with customers or developing your strategic vision. Just like acquiring intel, developing systems (especially in the early stages of your business) can feel like endless drudgery.

However, also like gathering intel, effort invested in developing well-refined systems is vital to creating sustainable success.

If you can't describe what you are doing as a process,
you don't know what you're doing.
— W. Edwards Deming

Operations? We Don't Need No Stinking Operations!

They may not be sexy or exciting, but certain operations are critical in order for your business to survive, let alone thrive. First, let's define what I mean by "operations." **Operations** are (for our purposes) the ongoing and repeatable activities that keep your business running smoothly. These activities include financial systems, lead generation and follow-through, inventory management, customer service, routine strategic planning, and anything else your business repeats with any degree of regularity throughout the day, week, month, quarter, or year.

In other words, "operations" encompasses just about everything you do to keep your business going!

Why are systems so important? Think of it this way: a football player very rarely reaches the end zone by himself; he has almost no chance if he tries to go it alone. In addition to the support of the other players around him, he has another team of supporting personnel: coaches, trainers, nutritionists, and analysts who serve as his intelligence-gatherers and go-to guys. Without all these systems functioning effectively in the background, even the all-star quarterback wouldn't have much hope for *survival* on the field, let alone scoring success.

Unfortunately, I see far too many entrepreneurs who lack even the "bare bones" skeleton of systemized operations. They may have an idea about how they should do things or even have it mapped out in their head, but they don't have an Operations Manual that details the various processes of their organization.

A shocking number of entrepreneurs lack even the "bare bones" skeleton of systemized operations.

You need to have at least a basic understanding of every department and function of your organization. As your operation grows in size and complexity, it becomes harder for you to keep tabs on every detail of what's happening. Greater complexity means you won't be an expert on everything, but the systems you put in place will provide you a working understanding of all the moving parts in your business.

You might be thinking "is this really so important...? I'm growing sales and bringing in money ... won't the back-office stuff just take care of itself?"

★ E-INSIGHT ★

Some Systems Aren't Sexy. Still...

Back-office systems don't get a lot of notoriety or front-page press. That's part of the reason why many entrepreneurs tend to ignore them. We want to go out and *achieve* (which isn't a bad thing). We want to be the one driving the hot new idea that's changing the way people think about ____. We want to mix it up, challenge the competition, and engage our customers in new, exciting ways!

So... for most of us, dealing with this systems stuff isn't very exciting.

It helps to think of it this way—once you've got your support systems in place and functioning properly, you'll have a lot more freedom to focus on building your business and providing targeted strategic direction for your team members—and that's why you're there.

Your *systems* allow you to accomplish the things you really want to accomplish. Ignore them and you'll end up in serious trouble!

Dream on! Unfortunately, I know from painful personal experience that trying to operate any company without proper systems—whether it's a solo professional practice or a complex multi-site, multi-state organization—is akin to wandering through a minefield with a blindfold on. Sometimes you get lucky, but sooner or later, you're going to step on something mighty unpleasant—and the results can be disastrous.

The good news is that the benefits of taking the time and energy to create and implement (and occasionally tweak) systems are legion.

Systemized operations:

- ★ Yield greater profits;
- ★ Enable better customer service;
- ★ Support more targeted marketing efforts;
- ★ Provide stronger team management; and
- ★ Ultimately, provide a significantly higher valuation should your exit strategy include a buyout or IPO.

Let's look at a prime example, one that all *successful* entrepreneurs experience: the "***Big Sale***."

A large influx of money from a major contract hits the top line, but your actual *profit* turns out far lower than anticipated. So where did the money go? For entrepreneurs without effective cash flow management systems, the usual answer is, "I have no idea!"

I've personally worked with numerous entrepreneurs who had great top line numbers (in the 7-figure range and beyond) and whose bottom line numbers were *really* bad. Their business was riddled with money leaks and they were paying everyone but themselves. Don't fall into that trap!

When you have clear, repeatable systems in place for handling incoming funds, you can track exactly where, when, and how money moves through your company. For instance, you might find a hidden "money leech" in the form of unnecessary expenses, higher-than-expected travel costs, or outsourcing overrides that siphon off your profit. With the right system in place, you can quickly identify the leech and pour a liberal dose of strategic salt on it.

But, trust me: without good systems in place, the money leeches will eventually bleed you dry!

Solid systems are also a great way to reinforce gaps and inherent strengths in your skill set, allowing you to focus your energy on your strongest facets. Let's say you're great at getting clients to "yes," quickly closing sales *if* you can get in front of the client. But, if you aren't terribly strong in managing lead generation or sales call follow-up, do you think you're going to land deals without having a good system in place? Maybe, maybe not, but how much *more* effective will you be with a targeted lead generation system and a highly-automated follow-up system supporting your efforts?

Without good systems in place, the money leeches will eventually bleed you dry.

Such systems (which can easily be run by a qualified virtual team member) free you to focus on your "Top 20," your areas of highest, and best time and energy use. Your team and supporting systems generate the leads, set the appointments, gather the pertinent pre-meeting intel and then initiate the post-call follow-up system, based on the outcome of the initial meeting. You are now free of the constant struggle of front- and back-end sales cycle management, enabling you to tackle more valuable strategic projects.

The long-term result? Greater revenue, increased profits, a well-functioning team, and one happy entrepreneur; one who isn't stuck in the weeds. You spend your time working *on* your business, not *in* your business. Sounds pretty good, right?

It *is* pretty good, but there's still that pesky short-term challenge of investing the time and effort to build these systems on the front-end. I won't lie to you: it's not easy for most entrepreneurs to get past their initial inertia and put these critical systems into place. But the good news is that others have already done much of the work for you (more on that later) and the advantages of having these systems in place far outweigh the temporary inconvenience of creating them.

One of the best reasons for systemizing as many aspects of your business as possible is that it allows you to concentrate on building a business that adds value to people's lives: your clients/customers, your team members, your family, and ultimately, your own life. Too many entrepreneurs spend all their time with their heads down, working under the hood, treating their companies as "the place I work" instead of creating something with lasting significance. I think it's important for entrepreneurs to spend a bit of time thinking about the end game—their exit strategy—when beginning their companies.

If you are currently in business and someone walked up to you on the street and offered you ten times your trailing 12-month revenue (a very generous offer) to purchase your business lock, stock, and barrel on the condition that it was a turnkey operation—all ready to go—would you be able to accept? Are the systems running in your company right now robust enough for a new owner to quickly understand how the business works? For the vast majority of entrepreneurs, the answer is a resounding "NO!" Yet these *systems must* be in place, clearly defined, and well understood by key people in your organization—even if you have no plans to sell.

Finally, effective systems provide you with the freedom to step away for a week or even a month with full confidence your business will continue running smoothly and producing revenue while you're gone. The earlier you start systemizing, the easier it is to keep everything under control, so don't put it off! In the next section, I'll share some tips on how to systemize your operations, and delve deeper into the benefits of getting started immediately.

The best time to plant a tree is 20 years ago.
The next best time is now!
— Chinese Proverb

The Time to Start Is Now

The best time to do the right thing – in your business as in life – is as soon as possible. I strongly encourage my start-up mastermind members to begin building their business systems right from Day One. Those already running an established business obviously can't start from the beginning, but they can start *today*. Avoid trying to get caught up on old data and filing systems before implementing your new ones; this will only slow you down. Instead, get your new system in place, and use some of the time freed up by new efficiencies to address these legacy issues over time.

So where do you begin? Each business is unique, so I can't give you absolute specifics on every system your company needs. However, there are three critical areas in which you must commit to developing good operations:

1. Cash flow
2. Professional operations
3. Personnel

Cash flow

I cannot stress enough the importance of understanding your cash flow. At the most basic level, you need to know how much money's coming in and where it ends up. Unfortunately, many of the entrepreneurs I connect with don't have a solid handle on their cash flow. They may have a ballpark idea of how much is coming in the front door, but have no knowledge of where it goes afterward and don't have a clue whether it's being spent effectively or not.

For example, say you don't have a system to track where your customers come from or how they find you. This means you can't tell which of the seven forms of advertising you're using delivers the highest return. Just by adding a single question— "How did you hear about us?"—to your intake process, you may discover 90 percent of your new business comes from just two of your seven advertising channels. Tracking this allows you to execute the best deployment strategy for your advertising dollars, ditching the deadweight methods, and shifting resources to your key promotional channels.

Cash-flow systems also help you to keep detailed, accurate records, which is always very important at tax time. Obviously, you want to avoid any trouble with local, state and federal tax agencies for failing to properly handle income or payroll taxes, while simultaneously taking advantage of every *legitimate* deduction you can.

Professional operations

Systems that fall under professional operations include a wide range of topics such as opening or closing your office or storefront (if you have a physical location) and how you onboard new subscribers or clients, to how to disseminate information within your organization and how to handle potential legal disputes.

I'm a firm believer in sharing information among team members who are affected, or potentially affected, by the information. Decide for yourself how you will disseminate key internal information. Will you send memos via email? Do intra-office webinars? Video chats? Or how about an old-fashioned face to face, in-person meetings? Personally, I enjoy a good meeting. When it's run properly and follows an agenda, a meeting can be engaging, informative, and action-driven. Run poorly, meetings are a complete waste of everyone's time. Do yourself and your team a favor and learn how to run a great meeting!

Many entrepreneurs unknowingly expose themselves to unnecessary legal liability. You might be relying on decades-old contracts with outdated language or be out of compliance with local, state, or federal regulatory requirements for your industry.

Regular check-ups with a legal advisor can easily confirm whether or not you are in compliance with any new laws, using the most up-to-date documents and ensuring adequate legal protection for yourself and your business. Without the correct system in place, these check-ups won't happen and important items

© 2018 Larry Broughton

can slip through the cracks all too easily. Often, you're unaware of any problems ... until you get sued. You might be completely innocent, but you'll still end up paying the price if you don't have the proper legal protections or insurance in place.

In addition, you also need a system to ensure that any ***other*** businesses with which you enter into a joint venture with are also up-to-date on all of these things. Otherwise, you could be held liable if they get sued while you're working on a joint project!

Personnel

While attending the Executive Program at Stanford University some 20 years ago, one of my professors often reminded us that the role of CEOs and entrepreneurs is to be problem solvers. He said that all business problems fall in to four categories: People Problems, Product Problems, Process Problems, and Profit Problems.

He explained struggles with R&D or product development; systems and operations, inventory control or supply chain process issues; or cash flow, departmental, or Gross Operating Profit problems; and that when we peel back the layers, we'll find that we really have a ***people problem***. He asserted that ***all*** problems in business are People Problems. If there are process problems in our organization, we likely have the wrong person developing and overseeing systems and operations; and if we have product problems, we likely need to replace the person overseeing R&D, or Q/A functions.

In the best-selling business bible, *Good to Great,* former Stanford professor and Socratic business consultant Jim Collins encourages leaders to get the right people on the right seat on the bus. When he speaks about the "bus," he's referring to making sure the team members are actually a great fit for the organization by sharing the core values and believing in the vision and mission. Which speaks to having team members work in their strengths. Have I hit you over the head enough on this strengths-based concept?

Since all problems within a business are actually people problems, getting a handle on your personnel system is vital. Key questions to consider when developing your personnel system include:

★ What is your hiring process?
★ How do you determine the requisite qualifications for each position?
★ How and when do you administer strengths assessments?
★ What is your probation or introductory period?

★ How do you conduct performance reviews?

★ How do you factor compensation packages?

Your personnel systems should also answer specific questions about job performance metrics. How will you determine whether a certain position is bringing value to your organization? Many companies have no system in place to measure this.

It can be daunting to think about building all these different systems from scratch. Fortunately, if you invest some exploratory time—if you gather your intel—you'll discover that many of the systems you need already exist and are successfully supporting businesses just like yours. Examples include:

★ Computer systems (networking, mobility)

★ Specialized software programs (communications, accounting)

★ Human resources manuals (training programs, leadership)

★ Consulting agreement templates (and templates for other important documents)

★ Virtual call centers (to answer your phone with a live human voice)

★ Client relationship management (CRM) systems (track all kinds of account data)

★ Lead generation and new business development systems (auto-follow-ups, prospecting services)

In fact, about 90 to 95 percent of the systems you need to start or grow your business are already available "off the shelf" and require little to no customization. You, and/or your team, simply need to put a little time into tweaking the last few pieces – those specific to your business.

The vast majority of systems you need are already available.

I routinely see entrepreneurs get overwhelmed by spending way too much time, energy, and money trying to reinvent the wheel. This approach is exhausting and unnecessary, so don't do it! Speak with others in your industry to see what they're using, reach out to your coach or mentor for recommendations and hire a knowledgeable consultant for a few hours to draft up a strategic systems plan. Trust me, the vast majority of what you need is already out there—you just need to invest some properly channeled time and energy to find it.

Another costly long-term error many entrepreneurs seem to make is automatically defaulting to the lowest-cost version available for each system they implement. While it's clearly understandable (it does cost money to purchase software or hire a systems consultant), this poverty mindset can really hurt you in the long run. Before finalizing your purchase decision, ask yourself these questions:

★ How much money am I willing to waste by *not* having the right systems in place?"

★ How much time am I going to throw away repeating the same tasks over again?"

★ How much do I stand to lose if I open myself up to a lawsuit because my contracts aren't up to date, or my personnel manual violates state law?"

Remember that purchasing, developing, and implementing the right systems is an investment in the success of your business, not an expense. In addition, enormous strides are taking place almost daily in scalable, highly-customizable technology solutions that allow you to run most businesses from anywhere in the world with just a smartphone, a laptop, and a reliable internet connection.

I place a lot of emphasis on getting good systems in place early, because I've learned the hard way how costly it is *not* to have them. I've also seen firsthand the opportunities that open up once they *are* in place, and we'll explore some of these opportunities in the next section.

A company can seize extraordinary opportunities only if
it is very good at the ordinary operations.
— Marcel Telles

Good Systems Produce Great Opportunities

The number one reason most entrepreneurs go into business is to create a good life for their families. Earlier in the chapter, you saw how implementing systems will make you more profitable, enable you to track your cash flow, and prevent the money leeches from draining your profits. You also learned how automating these systems will save you a substantial amount of time in the long run. The end results? Systems actually allow you to *enjoy* a better life with your family, not spending it at the office.

Let's step back and look at the bigger picture for a moment. Pardon me for being morbid, but what would happen if you weren't around to run your business? If you get hit by a bus on your way to work tomorrow, would your business grind to a halt? For many entrepreneurs, the answer is "yes." If the intimate knowledge of how your business runs is locked up exclusively in your own brain, no one else can truly step in to make your business work. You might have the best team in the world, but if they have to come to you for all the answers, they're dead in the water the minute you're not around.

Without documented, repeatable systems in place, whoever steps in to run your company is at a serious disadvantage. Imagine your spouse or children trying to pick up the pieces to keep your company going. Obviously, you'd want to provide them with every opportunity to succeed. In this worst-case scenario, good systems are a reliable way to provide for your family—even after you're gone.

Systems maximize the value of your company in the event someone wants to buy it.

But let's assume you *will* be around for a long time. The best way to take advantage of opportunities that may come your way is to have effective systems in place. Why? Because they maximize the value of your company in the event someone wants to buy it. You can seriously undercut the value of your company by not implementing good systems. Systems that exist only in your head aren't very attractive to buyers; many will shy away from companies that don't have documented systems in place.

★ E-INSIGHT ★

Buy the Systems, Too

Understanding the value of systems is just as important if you plan to purchase an existing company. Ensure that you fully investigate the organization's systems from top to bottom. If you discover there's nothing under the hood, either walk away or negotiate a deeply discounted price.

Also, make sure your purchase agreement stipulates you're buying all the systems that come with that company. If needed, negotiate with the previous owner (and/or other key personnel) to stay on board for a set period of time to train you in using the business's essential systems. You can ask for the previous owner stay for a week, a month, or whatever period of time you feel is necessary. The main thing is that you fully understand the systems of your new business so you can hit the ground running.

Others will make lowball offers for your business due to the extra risk involved in acquiring a company with anemic systems. Therefore, if part of your exit strategy is to sell your company, it is absolutely *critical* that you create and maintain superior systems to support it.

I once sold a hotel to a woman who had made a lot of money in a big real estate deal. That one deal made her an "expert" (at least in her mind) and she approached our deal with an "I already know everything" attitude. During our negotiations, I offered to include all the systems that went with the property—the website, operations manuals, training guides, reservation system, and the pictography—and her response? "I don't need any of that ... I don't want any of it."

I strongly encouraged—almost begged—her to take the systems as part of the business. But she adamantly refused. I don't know if she simply didn't understand how critical the established systems, manuals, and guides were to her success, or if she just had bad advisors around her. What I *do* know is that the hotel's revenue and market share declined rapidly, the key team members left for jobs elsewhere, negative guest complaints started appearing across the online review sites, and she lost money on the hotel – she eventually sold it for far less than she paid me.

Learn from her mistake. Make sure you buy the systems that control the company's operation. If you find a company you want to acquire does not have those systems in place, that company is worth much, much less, because it's going to take a lot more time, work, and money for you to bring it up to speed.

★ VICTORY SUCCESS STORY ★

One of the biggest "ah ha" moments I had reading VICTORY *was just how much of my business was in my head. And, because it was in my head, it was hard to share it with my team when they needed it. It also explained why I was so frustrated when my team didn't always do things the way I wanted them done.*

Dan Spangler
Owner/CEO
A Dog's Dream Pet Resort

I realized that not having written things down was causing us to fail, even though it didn't look like it. That was one of the hardest things for me to understand about this. I had been in business a couple of years, and things were going well, but not as well as it could have been, because we didn't have things like guidelines and procedures memorialized. Yes, the business was operating, but was it operating optimally? It just wasn't.

Larry encouraged me to create a systems manual. I'm not a natural systems guy, so a friend of mine (who is brilliant at creating systems) offered to come out to our facility in North Carolina to create an operations manual with me.

When we sat down to write everything out, we realized there was a lot of detail to many of the procedures. A lot of what we do has to be done "just so" for compliance purposes, so we thought, why don't we just videotape it? We pulled out a video camera and started recording. Instead of writing two pages about how to unlock the building and turn off the alarm system we videotaped for two minutes and had a full video that anyone on the team can watch. In one weekend, we created about 50 videos that covered nearly every routine aspect of my business, from checking in dogs to cleaning out the sink in the grooming area.

Then we took "hot topics" suggested by my team of questions they had, and we made short, one- to five-minute videos. At first, I was worried about having things perfect—the right lighting, the perfect camera, a rehearsed script—but it's so much easier and more realistic to just do it. As business owners, we can wait until things are perfect or we can take action and do something. My video systems manual isn't perfect, or professionally edited, but the main points are in there. I've updated them since they were first created and we're up to 65 videos now. As new team members come on board, they can watch the videos—it helps cut down on training time and ensures more consistent customer care.

The process of creating the video systems manual was incredibly helpful to see where my team needed guidance and to standardize daily procedures and processes for all team members. I got my team involved by asking them what questions they always get from clients and created an "FAQ" video series. And, I found that the way I wanted certain things done—something as simple as answering the phone in a professional manner—isn't the way other people naturally do things.

Our video systems manual has increased efficiency, improved customer care and retention, and cut down on my having to answer the same questions over and over. When they know how to answer the clients' questions, it also makes my team look like more of the experts in dog care the clients expect.

Now, it's your turn! Share your *VICTORY* success story with me at success@larrybroughton.me. I'd love to hear from you!

True business owners can go on vacation forever
because they own a system, not a job.
— Robert Kiyosaki

★ ACTION STEP: START YOUR SYSTEMS ★

Part 1: Look back at Column 1 (*"Doing"*) of the 3-Column Exercise in the previous chapter. Find the task item you enjoy the least or procrastinate on the most. This is an ideal target for systemization. Decide what you want the outcome to be and how you can delegate, delete, or outsource this task to achieve your desired outcome.

Part 2: For each of the main systems categories discussed in this chapter— cash flow, professional operations, and personnel—write down the routine tasks, procedures and/or guidelines that occur in each category. Ask your team for the questions they're most often asked by clients.

Part 3: Develop a plan to create an entry in your systems manual for each item identified in #2 above. Take out your smartphone right now and record an audio or video of you explaining at least one item.

_____

_____

_____

_____

CHAPTER  6
RAPID ACTION

A good plan violently executed today is better than a perfect plan next week.

Gen. George F. Patton, Jr.

You've been lied to from a very young age. You've probably heard the expression "knowledge is power." It's an old saying, and many people still believe it. There's just one small problem: *it's a lie*. Don't believe it for a second!

The truth is that inspired and decisive *action* is power. If you could hook your brain up to the Library of Congress (one of the largest repositories of data in the world) and download every bit of information residing there, and you did nothing with all that knowledge, all you would have is useless trivia. But, if you took action with that newfound knowledge, you'd be an absolute powerhouse!

Key Challenge

Too many entrepreneurs spin their wheels, rev their engines, and wait for just the right opportunity to move. They wait for just a *little* more information, to put the finishing touches on their formal business plans or websites, maybe for the perfect alignment of the stars. Who knows? But they wait. Six months, a year, or even more will pass by and they're still stuck in neutral, because something prevents them from getting in gear, taking action, and driving forward.

I cannot overstress the importance of taking rapid action. Not just action—*rapid* action. That's why one of my favorite quotes from General George Patton opens this chapter. General Patton doesn't talk about an awesome plan. He doesn't talk about a stellar plan. He didn't even talk about a great plan. What he talks about is a good plan *violently executed* today is better than a perfect plan next week. How often have we gotten stuck in life because we're trying to strive for perfection? Or our business plan isn't just so, or our marketing plan isn't just right, or that perfect person hasn't walked into our life and become our new life partner.

How often do we just get stuck expecting that perfection is going to solve all our problems?

What is not started will never get finished.
— Johann Wolfgang von Goethe

Success is for *Doers*, Not Dreamers

Action delivers results. Action creates opportunities. Action dampens potential blowback from the occasional (and inevitable) error. Taking rapid, decisive action is the single greatest differentiator between barely surviving and truly thriving.

History is replete with the exploits of legendary leaders who took decisive action, including Alexander the Great, Julius Caesar, Horatio Nelson, Robert E. Lee, Henry Ford, Andrew Carnegie, George S. Patton, Jr., Dr. Martin Luther King, Jr., Elon Musk, Mark Cuban, and Barbara Corcoran. Through their exploits—their *actions*—they overcame the challenges they faced as well as their opponents and rivals.

Conversely, leaders whose vacillation, dithering, and endless indecision reduced them to historical footnotes. Feckless unfortunates such as Darius III of Persia, Guy d' Lusignan, Antonio Lopez De Santa Anna, George B. McClellan, Ambrose Burnside, Douglas Haig, and Maurice Gamelin provide stark reminders of failure and ineptitude.

I routinely interact with top achievers in many different industries. These men and women create enormous positive change, run great organizations, achieve explosive growth, and are continually innovating. They don't have much in common on the outside; their heights, weights, ethnicities, political beliefs, and levels of education are all different. But there's a single, salient strength that ties these top achievers together: the ability to *get things done*.

The ability to take rapid, decisive action is more important than intelligence, education, and even raw talent. In many ways, it is the single best predictor of the level of success you will achieve, both in business and in life.

I often find entrepreneurs idling at the starting line, waiting on some external factor, such as government approval for a big contract, the bank finalizing a financing package, or a team member finishing a proposal. They get completely fixated on breaking through this single perceived barrier to moving their business forward, and everything grinds to a halt.

You need to take action in your business and life because, quite frankly, nobody owes you anything. This includes the government, your employer, your clients/customers, and your spouse or significant other. No one is going to solve your problems for you; sitting around waiting for your white knight to turn up is futile. The only way to solve a challenge, create or take advantage of an opportunity, and ultimately reach your goals is to get yourself in gear and *take action*.

Sound a bit harsh? Good…it's meant to!

Please don't confuse my "nobody owes you anything" comment above with operating the Lone Wolf way. It's easy to conflate the two, but the most common action step I recommend when mentoring a "stuck" entrepreneur is to engage outside help to shift perspective and reframe the challenge.

Sitting around waiting for your white knight to turn up is futile.

Our culture celebrates dreamers. The self-help shelves at bookstores are packed with titles, all directing us to follow our dreams. I get it—that's why Chapter One of this book focuses on **Vision**. It's dreamers who envision the transformative ideas that lead to great advancements in every area of business and life. That said, dreaming alone isn't enough, and a quick look at any leading change agent reveals the decisive actions they took to turn their dreams into reality.

★ E-INSIGHT ★

System Shock

Most entrepreneurs are shocked by the staggering volume of information, issues, and challenges they must now deal with on any given business day (and during their off-hours, too). Whether you're starting up straight out of school or you're making the shift from corporate, government, or other employment, you're probably not used to dealing with myriad responsibilities that come with entrepreneurship. You'll have to adopt a *completely new mindset* – which explains why getting stuck can be so easy!

It will probably take some time for you to get into your entrepreneurial groove. But even the best musicians hit a sour note once in a while – so fight the urge to get too down on yourself and don't allow negative self-talk to creep in. Entrepreneurship is tough enough without beating yourself up over it!

Entrepreneurs must be doers as well as dreamers. The transition can be a real challenge if you're coming from a W-2 paycheck environment, where you receive a regular paycheck even if you aren't working all that hard to earn it. Sometimes when you're in a safe/comfortable corporate or government job, it's easy to get a little lazy (don't tell anyone, but I've been there too). But no more! As an entrepreneur, you don't have the luxury of slacking off, because your income is directly related to the amount of positive activity in which you engage. Simply put, if you get lazy as an entrepreneur, you end up with no food on the table!

"Taking action" means more than just initiating projects and activities. Completing actions, closing the loop, and crossing them off your to-do list are all crucial. This is a major challenge for many entrepreneurs who are great idea *generators*, but who aren't as strong when it comes to idea *completion*. Entrepreneurs in general suffer from the "bright shiny object" syndrome … it's part of our DNA (and as a charter member of the Bright Shiny Object Club, I'm intimately familiar with this syndrome).

If you get lazy as an entrepreneur, you end up with no food on the table.

Ever start one project and pursue it with boundless energy … until another bright, shiny object catches your eye? Poof! Instant distraction! So, you dive into your new project … until the next shiny object appears. It's a vicious cycle and it can easily lead you to build an impressive portfolio of brilliant, but half-completed, projects without ever actually accomplishing anything.

This pattern poses several significant dangers. First, these partial projects are rarely profitable and each represents a lost opportunity for income, building credibility in your industry, or making your business more efficient. Entrepreneurs who fall victim to this common pattern often have careers consisting of one unrealized opportunity after another because they simply don't see any one opportunity through to the finish line.

The second danger is what I call "entrepreneurial brain drain." Each activity you leave unfinished creates what psychologists call an "open loop" in your mind. You'll keep thinking about an unfinished task whether you notice or not, even when you're working on something else. Each unfinished task siphons

THE ENTREPRENEUR'S PATH

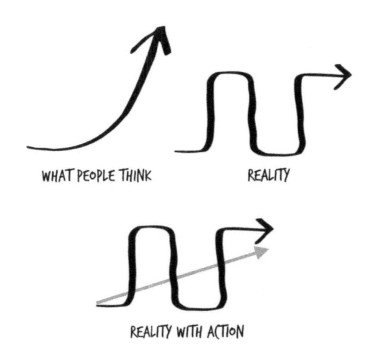

WHAT PEOPLE THINK   REALITY

REALITY WITH ACTION

© 2018 Larry Broughton

off some of your cognitive ability, creates background noise in your subconscious, and lowers your ability to focus on your current project. The more open loops from unfinished projects, the greater the brain drain and noise level until eventually, this effect completely short-circuits your ability get things done.

The best way to avoid entrepreneurial brain drain is to complete one task before moving on to the next. That's easier said than done, given our modern propensity for multi-tasking, but bringing maximum mental firepower to bear on a task before moving on can make a huge impact on your productivity. While shifting to an action-oriented mindset is essential, *completing* those actions is even more important to your long-term success.

If you aren't accustomed to taking action; if you're more comfortable thinking, pondering, and contemplating until the spirit moves you, then developing an action-oriented mindset is going seem strange to you at first. But don't worry—you'll grow into it.

Ever gone running or skiing, or played a game of volleyball on the beach? Your first time is often very uncomfortable. Your legs hurt, you can barely breathe, and you're sore the next day. But if you keep it up, your muscles start to grow and adapt, your cardiopulmonary system responds, and before long you're stronger and faster thanks to the effort you put into developing your exciting new skill.

The same thing happens when you start taking action. You might feel awkward or unprepared as you first move out towards achieving your goals, but you will get more comfortable. Every success (and the lessons you learn from occasional misfires) increases your confidence and comfort level with taking decisive action. Soon, you'll discover you look at things in an entirely different way: with an action-oriented mindset.

This action-oriented mindset is a huge component of your success. But what if you're already primed for action and unsure of which action to take? The next section is for you.

Achievement seems to be connected with action. Successful men and women keep moving. They make mistakes, but they don't quit.
— *Conrad Hilton*

Acting in The Face of Uncertainty

Wouldn't it be great if you had a clearly-defined goal and perfect line of sight *before* taking action, every time? Unfortunately, today's dynamic business world offers few perfect views and even fewer sure things. You've already seen how waiting for the perfect stellar alignment is a direct route to the poor house; you must develop some degree of comfort with moving out and taking course-corrective action as you go forward.

Of course, you won't be taking action blindly if you've given some thought to the principles I've covered in this book. I trust you've already applied some brainpower to:

- ★ Developing the vision for your organization
- ★ Researching and analyzing appropriate intel
- ★ Connecting with coaches/mentors
- ★ Building your custom-designed support team
- ★ Getting the right systems in place to support your growth

At some point though, you must stop analyzing, and start doing! I talk to far too many entrepreneurs trapped in "analysis paralysis," struggling to get into action mode. They have reams of information and multiple courses of action swirling around in their heads, but don't know what to do with it all. Trying to pick the right target when you're stuck in entrepreneurial overwhelm, to be frank, simply sucks. I've been there multiple times in my extensive business career.

So, what should you do? My advice is to simply get moving! Connect with your vision, goals, and intel to determine your starting point and initial direction and ***get on it***. Focus your marketing on those you believe are most interested in your product or service (just remember, target what they ***want***, not what you think they ***need***). Look for low-hanging fruit and take on targets of opportunity as you go. People are often surprised at how easily they gain clients/customers once they get into action.

As you're rolling, take note of what's working and what isn't. Refine your message or shift your efforts to zero in on your most receptive audience, and discard preconceived notions that don't pan out. This "build the airplane as you fly" approach is incredibly uncomfortable for some entrepreneurs, but it's critically important, especially if you're in start-up or rapid growth mode.

This approach is the business equivalent of a military tactic known as "recon by fire." In combat, when a unit believes a certain area to be a likely enemy position, the unit may open fire hoping to provoke the enemy into revealing their true position with a reaction. As an entrepreneur, sometimes you must use exactly the same tactic. If you believe you can successfully compete in a market segment, you need to engage that segment.

★ E-INSIGHT ★

The Perfect Time for Action

I'd like to ask a simple question. Is now the perfect time to take action? Absolutely not! There's no such thing as the *perfect time* to do most anything. Perfectionism is the mortal enemy of the entrepreneur, and those who attempt to attain it end up mighty sorry they did. Trust me: even if you manage to craft the perfect plan and arrange perfect circumstances, they'll only stay perfect on paper. Any plan starts breaking down the moment you implement it and make contact with external forces. There's a great quote from a 19th century Prussian general: "No battle plan survives contact with the enemy."

This is just as true in business as in battle. You'll need to improvise, adapt and take course-corrective actions continuously. Maybe you'll make a quick adjustment, a lane change, or a complete U-turn. Figure it out in mid-stride and *keep moving*. If you stop every ten feet to reanalyze everything, others will fly past you in terms of success.

They may not be as smart as or well-educated as you. They may not have your network, financial backing, or support systems. Their product/service might not be nearly as good as yours. But if they've developed an action-oriented mindset and are continuously moving forward, they will consistently beat you to market and co-opt your clients/customers. All because they initiated their imperfect plan and took decisive action!

Engaging your market can take many forms, depending on your resources, skill set, support team, and the market itself. Focused (and low-cost) marketing, speaking appearances, and joint ventures with complementary businesses already enjoying success in the market are all solid strategies. If you're correct and it *is* a target-rich environment, your message will start resonating and gaining traction, allowing you to expand your business.

I want to speak now to the part of your brain that's screaming, "But what if I'm wrong?!" The fear of making mistakes is one of the biggest reasons entrepreneurs refrain from taking action. It really shouldn't be, because failure is an important ingredient of success. This may sound counter-intuitive, but it's absolutely true. When you fail in business (and remember, you <u>will</u> fail), it simply means you tried something that didn't work. So, learn from your mistake, adjust accordingly, and try again! Most highly successful entrepreneurs freely admit they learned far more from their failures than from their successes.

As an entrepreneur, you shouldn't be too afraid of failure in business; it's rarely a life-and-death affair. Sure, you might lose some money, some respect, or a little dignity—you can recover from all of those. Take failure for what it really is: the opportunity to learn, expand and take advantage of your new knowledge.

In reality, fear of failure is misplaced fear. The only thing you should fear is inaction. You can recover from your mistakes. You can regroup, analyze what went wrong, and make course corrections. But if you do nothing, I guarantee you'll miss every opportunity for success that comes your way. You don't want to look back over your life and wonder, "what might have happened if only I had...?"

It's easy to make a habit out of letting fear hold you back. The good news is that taking action is also very habit-forming, because habits are like muscles:

they don't start out strong—you don't just wake up one morning and start bench-pressing 300 pounds. You work your muscles vigorously and consistently, and before long you notice the difference in your strength level.

Action creates and attracts opportunities.

Your "action habit muscle" follows the same principle. Even if it's not that strong right now, the more you exercise it the more powerful it becomes. Of course, for most of us, the hardest part of any exercise program is actually getting started—taking that first action. In the next section, I'll share three simple exercises to help you quickly build your action habit muscles—and keep them strong.

Remember, fortune favors those who take action. You will find opportunity by moving out and staying true to your vision and values, even if it's not the kind you originally expected. I personally know scores of entrepreneurs who started moving down the entrepreneurial road with one concept in mind and discovered a far more lucrative opportunity right around the first bend.

Unfortunately, I also know a fair number who just sit on the side of the road, convinced of the brilliance of their own ideas and waiting for the business to come to them. Honestly, no amount of positive thinking or self-affirmation is going to cause opportunities to fall from the sky and drop into your lap (no matter what the Law of Attraction says). Action both creates and attracts opportunities.

You might be thinking, "Great, Larry … I get that I need to develop an action-oriented mindset, but how? How do I overcome my analysis paralysis and fear of failure and start moving forward, making my company vision a reality?"

I'm glad you asked! In the next section I'm giving you three simple principles you can apply every day to get yourself, and keep yourself, in action.

I never worry about action, but inaction.
— Sir Winston Churchill

Develop an Action Mindset

During my military career, I had the opportunity to jump out of perfectly good airplanes—Airborne parachute jumps! Of course, the military doesn't just take you up in a plane and throw you out. You go through weeks of proper training and ensure you have all the right moves, mindset, and equipment. You build your confidence through a series of small achievements until you're finally ready to board the plane for that first real jump. Once on the aircraft, you follow all the steps, movements, and commands you learned and practiced on the ground, until you ultimately shuffle to the door of the C-130 transport plane and then you … freeze. Even with all that training, preparation, and your previous successes, you still just freeze.

Many of you reading this have probably never been in such a high-stress, truly life or death situation, so trust me when I tell you that if you don't jump at exactly the right time, or you don't leave the aircraft with the proper body position, the results can be disastrous. You (and everyone behind you) could miss your drop zone. Your unit could become separated. You could even end up landing right on top of the enemy instead of with your own troops! That's why there's a firm and loving Jumpmaster in the plane to heave you respectfully out the door if necessary.

For this section, I'm going to be your jumpmaster—getting you out the door and into action with three simple—but enormously effective—principles. I've touched on these concepts throughout the chapter, and they are crucial for getting into action. The door's open ... let's jump!

★ **Principle #1—Seek Progress, Not Perfection:** Understand, accept, and internalize the fact that *there is no perfect plan*. Even your most meticulous plans won't survive exposure to the real world intact, so stop trying to be perfect! Get moving in the direction of making your vision a reality and always keep your head up, looking for opportunities. Strive for sustained progress and make course corrections as needed through the filters of your vision, your mentors, and your team.

Business today is so dynamic that the only constant is change. Technology, market and economic conditions, new applications for existing products/services, and the wants of clients and customers are always in motion. To succeed, you must be moving too!

★ **Principle #2—Don't Try to Eat the Elephant in One Bite:** We often fail to take action because the task before us seems too daunting, like trying to eat an entire elephant in one sitting. The solution? Try breaking seemingly overwhelming tasks into smaller chunks, and dig into the bite- sized pieces with gusto! Once you start knocking out the smaller pieces, you'll find your big task looks much less menacing. Also, don't be afraid to start with something small. Sometimes, just accomplishing something relatively simple, like making a phone call to schedule an appointment with a potential client, gives you the motivation you need to attack the larger project. Action fuels motivation!

★ **Principle #3—The More You Act, the Easier It Gets:** Developing your action habit muscle is just like any other strength or endurance-building exercise. The more you take action, the stronger you get, and the easier action becomes.

This is the primary reason breaking overwhelming tasks into bite-sized pieces works so well. You accomplish one small task, then another and another and before long, you'll notice you are thinking differently and actively looking for new reasons and ways to act, instead of making excuses for why you can't.

Refer to these three simple principles any time you feel yourself getting stuck or frustrated. Remember: aim for progress, not perfection; break large projects into bite-sized pieces; and the more you practice taking rapid, decisive action, the easier it becomes.

NOW GET MOVING!

★ VICTORY SUCCESS STORY ★

When I was growing up and wanted to excuse myself from the dinner table, I'd announce to whomever would listen, "I'm going to clean my room."

As often as I said that, you'd think I would have had the cleanest room on the block. I didn't. I'd get absorbed by the process of putting things away, stop to read a magazine, or try on an outfit from the clothes strewn around the room.

Deanne Marie
CEO | Creative Director
evolve Marketing | Design

My first business/side hustle was targeted to "busy people." I was busy: working long hours as an attorney, going to school at night for interior design, sitting on boards, organizing charity events, and still throwing parties, sending 100 Christmas cards a year and Martha Stewart-ing my home.

Reading VICTORY *and following Larry's advice challenged me to rethink being busy. What was I really doing? There's a difference between activity and action. For years I wondered why I felt like I was doing a lot, but accomplishing little. For me it wasn't about time management or productivity. It turned out, it was about making a decision to act.*

At Larry's behest, I did the Kolbe A and the StrengthsFinder assessments and discovered I'm naturally a thinker. A deep thinker. I like facts and investigation and turning things over in my head 25,000 times. All thought and no real action! It felt like the entrepreneurial equivalent of staying cozy in a warm bed on a dreary cold morning. You just don't want to move. It may feel cozy, but it's fatal to growth and more importantly, to momentum.

Once I saw and understood these things about myself, I could take the ideas and the vision, all the fact-finding intel, the input from my mentor (Larry) and mastermind, and finally act on it! I got an accountability partner—this is a necessity for someone like me—and I learned that once I get going, momentum kicks in and it helps me to keep moving forward. Action, even in the face of fear, is tremendously satisfying!

I think I was afraid that making a decision to take action on something meant I couldn't do anything else. Ever. But what I wasn't seeing was that the next step after taking action is assessment, and then course corrections can be made if needed. "Act and adjust" is my new mantra.

Without action, I was stuck. I had all the ingredients for entrepreneurial success, but I was just admiring them and staying cozy in bed. With consistent action, my business has evolved to use the best parts of my strengths and experience to serve world-class clients with their branding and copywriting.

> **Now, it's your turn! Share <u>your</u> *VICTORY* success story with me at success@larrybroughton.me. I'd love to hear from you!**

Well done is better than well said.
— Benjamin Franklin

★ ACTION STEP: TAKE ACTION NOW! ★

In **Principle #2** above, I recommend breaking overwhelming tasks down into bite-size chunks. One of the oldest, simplest, and most effective tools ever developed for getting things done is the humble "To-Do List."

Its power is underestimated, which is why few achievement and success *seekers* use it. Ask top *achievers* about the importance of a To-Do List, however, and you'll find few who can live without one. Just beware of getting overly enthusiastic about adding items to your list.

It's easy to feel overwhelmed and drained by too many tasks, which can lead to procrastination. Develop a list of all the items you need to complete in order to achieve your goals. Then, review your list and identify the top two or three projects that need your attention *right away*. Break these top items down into smaller, actionable pieces you can complete within the next 24 to 36 hours. Each time you complete a task, cross it off your list. Feels good, doesn't it?

Continually revise your list. Ask yourself if you really need to do *everything* on the list. Can you delegate anything on there? Put any new items on a separate to-do list. This list will be far less scary, making it easier to take action, and get things done.

CHAPTER 7

YOU

In reading the lives of great men, I found that the first victory they won was over themselves … self-discipline with all of them came first.

President Harry S. Truman

People naturally have greater respect for confident, disciplined, and self-directed people who are guided by their own conscience, rather than other-directed people who allow their lives to be guided according to the whims of others.

The self-directed achiever is not tossed about on the whims of what others think. They set their own goals and intentions, and then move in a predetermined direction. They're confident in their abilities and can't be easily led astray.

Conversely, the person who is consumed with negative self-talk and is not self-directed will often change their way of doing things according to the opinions of others, which will be rightfully seen as a lack of self-confidence. This often becomes what is known as a "self-fulfilling prophecy."

This chapter is devoted to the most important aspect of your business: YOU. We'll dive deep into what makes you tick, and how you can be the best version of yourself.

Key Challenge

The very qualities that make entrepreneurs great leaders—hard-working, driven, curious, creative—can consume our time and energy, leaving little left over at the end of day for our loved ones and our own-well being. And, I've seen over and over how the desire to succeed can result in little ethical wobbles that, left unchecked, eventually have the power to destroy businesses and relationships, and land once well-meaning entrepreneurs in trouble with the law.

Greatness is not a function of circumstance. Greatness, it turns out, is largely a matter of conscious choice and discipline.
— Jim Collins

It's All About You

The first six strategies you learned (Vision, Intel, Coaching, Team Building, Operations, and Rapid Action) are essential elements of building long-term success in business. But unless you also apply the ideas outlined in this chapter, the other strategies won't matter. When you strip everything else away, your success—in your business and your life—depends on *you*.

You can think of the other strategies as spokes in a wheel. You are the hub of that wheel: no matter how strong the spokes are, any wheel will eventually break down if the hub isn't sound. In this chapter, I'll share my perspective on what it takes to build a business, and a life, of long-lasting satisfaction and significance.

> ## When you strip away everything else, your success—in business and in life—depends on you.

Why have you chosen the entrepreneurial lifestyle? At the most basic level, of course, most of us desire to create a stream of income that supports the kind of life we want for our families (and ourselves). Many of us also want to help support the charities and causes we believe in. Finally, the majority of us have a genuine desire to use our experience and talents to help make a positive difference in the world around us.

When you look at the sacrifice and dedication it takes to successfully start and grow a business, it's obvious there's more involved than just making a living. After all, you're willingly signing up for a rollercoaster ride of peaks and valleys, victories and defeats, frustration and euphoria … and that's before breakfast each morning!

Why? What drives us to do what we do? The assessment tools I discussed earlier in the book (the _Kolbe A_ Index and the _CliftonStrengths_) are great starting points to figure out what really motivates you.

This also ties into the vision you have for your organization, as well as your personal vision for your life. Review your company and personal vision statements regularly. In fact, why not take a few moments and review them

---

★ E-INSIGHT ★

Clarity is Attractive

You should clearly communicate who you are and what you stand for to your potential customers and clients. It will resonate with many of them and your company will be much more attractive because of it.

What if you scare some of your customers off by talking openly about your values? You might. But your goal is to build a fiercely loyal customer base that connects with you on an emotional level. You can only achieve that by being open and transparent about what's important to *you* ... so that you can become important to *them*.

Remember that you've got to do more than pay lip service to your values. You've got to walk the walk, because potential customers *will* check you out to see if you're really doing business as you purport to be. This is an opportunity for you to build trust and confidence in your customer base by showing them you truly stand behind what you say.

---

right now? If you haven't fully developed them yet, just take five minutes to jot down some of your key thoughts.

Remember, vision is not something you think about once and stuff in your desk drawer, never to be looked at again. Keep your personal reasons for doing what you do front and center and refer to them often, especially when things get tough.

To achieve long-term success, you must understand the three priorities that virtually all high achievers have developed into routine habits. Connect with these priorities; make them second nature so they're always operating in the background of everything you do.

I believe keeping these priorities in mind can literally make you unstoppable … if you choose to embrace them:

★ **Self-discipline:** Self-discipline, in this context, means a number of different things. It means that once you start something, you *finish* it. You resist the bright shiny object syndrome that afflicts so many entrepreneurs (including me), because you know that maintaining your momentum is very difficult if you're easily distracted.

Self-discipline also means that you pursue excellence in everything you or your company does. The entrepreneurial lifestyle will *not* work for you if you think "mediocre" is "good enough." Committing to excellence builds customer loyalty, attracts world-class team members, and distinguishes you in a marketplace overwhelmingly flooded with "average."

At its core, self-discipline means making decisions based on what's right, not what feels good at the moment. The right decisions benefit your clients/customers and your team while honoring your vision and values— instead of sacrificing quality for expediency and convenience. Self-disciplined leaders make conscious, deliberate decisions and avoid cutting corners or compromising principles to squeeze a few extra dollars from a transaction.

★ **Tenacity:** Tenacity simply means *not giving up*, no matter the circumstance. Tenacity is refusing to allow opposition, uncertainty, and the occasional failure to keep you from succeeding. Any time you move forward and/or challenge the status quo, you're going to face adversity. The question is … what are you going to *do* about it?

When you encounter opposition, obstacles, or adversity, you have two options: you can quit (always the wrong choice) or you can regroup, learn from your mistakes, adjust your course by five or ten degrees, and push forward. It's too bad so many entrepreneurs are willing to throw in the towel the very first time they run into a real challenge.

I strongly believe that tenacity is part of what sets the world's most successful entrepreneurs apart from the rest, because we understand adversity and temporary failure only make us stronger. I've seen a meme circle around the social media platforms that says, "Failure is temporary, but quitting lasts forever."

★ **Commitment to self-development:** The skills and knowledge required to successfully navigate business startups are not the same skills needed to take that same business to the next level. If you're not continuously growing as a leader, you'll eventually stifle your own company's success. Don't be the anchor that weighs your company down: set the example through continuous development and growth.

How can you keep growing as a leader? You've got plenty of options. Commit to reading a certain number of leadership/business books per year. Listen to podcasts on your commute to and from work and while working out. Go to leadership seminars and retreats. Pursue a noteworthy professional designation in your industry. In reality, exactly how you do it is less important than your commitment to actually getting it done.

Investing in coaching and participating in mastermind groups are two of the best ways to enhance your skills. Find a coach who understands where you need to go as a leader, and who can help you get there. A good mastermind group will enable you to stretch, think, and grow. You'll find the money you invest in these programs is well spent, since you're investing in your most valuable business asset—you!

One final priority I strongly suggest establishing in your business from Day One is ***uncompromising ethics***. I encourage you to set and maintain the highest possible ethical standards for both yourself and your company; I've dedicated the following section to a detailed discussion on why.

The time is always right to do what is right.
— Martin Luther King

Maintain Your Moral Compass

Time magazine declared the first decade of the 21st century as the, "Decade from Hell." How did they come to this conclusion? One key factor was the extensive financial upheaval and corruption prevalent throughout the decade. Think Enron, WorldCom, the dot-com boom and subsequent bust, Lehmann Brothers, the housing bubble and mortgage fraud, Bernie Madoff, and a whole host of similar sordid characters. There are literally dozens of examples from this time period of people taking ethical shortcuts to obtain short-term "success," often destroying hundreds or even ***thousands*** of lives in the process.

Of course, the media and popular culture feeds right into the perception that all business owners are crooks, out for a quick buck at anyone's expense. In movies, business leaders are typically portrayed as one-dimensional villains looking to make money by any means available, legal or illegal.

Ethical lapses usually start small, but they tend to grow quickly.

In reality, business people who fit that description are quite rare. Most business owners care deeply about their customers. They also care about their employees—their team members—and are often actively involved in their communities and dedicated to their families. Unfortunately, the super-villain stereotypes still persist. A tiny fraction of unscrupulous business leaders allow their rotten ethical standards to pollute the reputation of the vast majority of honest, hard-working business leaders.

Based on my research and experience, many (if not most) of these disgraced business leaders started off as basically honest people. At some point, though, they chose to start cutting corners. Maybe they told a little white lie to a client to close a deal. Perhaps they took credit for something they didn't do to receive a promotion they didn't deserve. Ethical lapses usually start small, but they tend to grow quickly until they take over the life of the person committing them.

The best way to keep from going down that road is to set your moral and ethical standards at the very beginning of your career. You must decide from the start that you **will not** cut corners, no matter what.

This is where your ethical standards tie into the type of self-discipline I mentioned in the previous section. You cannot make decisions based on how you feel at the moment or what's expedient. Whatever your industry, business is a high-pressure game. You may be tempted to toss ethics out the window to make a quick sale, especially if your business is having a really tight month. Don't. You must commit, right from the start, that you will **always** occupy the highest moral ground.

You're going to find that if you do stick to the highest moral standard, people won't always understand what you're doing. Some business peers may even think you're foolish because you don't pad your invoices or undercut your competition with artificially low bids. What's right isn't always what's popular—challenge the status quo.

You also need to establish these same ethical standards in your team members. Stress the values important to your company, starting in the interview process. The best time to weed out people who won't uphold your ethical standards is **before** you hire them. If you discover one of your team members is cutting ethical corners, even in minor areas, don't ignore it. Looking the other way and hoping things will straighten themselves out rarely works. They won't! Deal with the situation swiftly and decisively.

It can be difficult to terminate—or even discipline—any team member, especially one who makes good money for the company. But minor ethical lapses are dangerous for a number of reasons. One reason is that a team member who will lie to or cheat a customer in order to gain an advantage will, given the chance, do the same thing to you. You may profit from this employee's misdeeds at first, but cleaning up their messes will end up costing you far more.

Although it's a very real aspect of the costs incurred through ethical lapse, money isn't all you stand to lose. These costs can also include lost customers (revenue), lawsuits, and most importantly, respect and credibility. When you lose the respect of your customers and peers, it's incredibly difficult (if not outright impossible) to get it back. This is *far* too high a price to pay just to make a quick buck.

To achieve enduring success, you must build it on a foundation of the highest ethical standards. People, customers and team members alike, want to attach themselves to a company that's clear about what it stands for and does what it says it will do. So far, many companies don't do a very good job of this, so you will stand out in your industry!

If you have integrity, nothing else matters.
If you don't have integrity, nothing else matters.
— Harvey MacKay

How Integrity Will Set You Apart
Now More Than Ever

From politicians who shamelessly lie (but keep getting elected) to careless business leaders who bankrupt their own companies (but still walk away with their millions), from sports heroes who display morals and values fit for a sociopath (but still keep their fans) to welfare cheats who rip-off the system (but are never punished), the very concept of integrity seems to be at odds with today's "modern" society.

So, with seemingly *everyone* lying, cheating, and stealing … is integrity dead?

If you're in any sort of leadership position—and want to remain there for any length of time—the answer is a resounding "NO!"

I opened this section with a famous quote from Harvey MacKay, the business guru and author of five best-selling books (including *Swim with the Sharks*). Go back and read it again, and let it sink in.

Integrity, according to the first definition in the dictionary, is "the quality of being honest and having strong moral principles."

It's routinely the most important value listed by clients, customers, suppliers, supervisors, and team members when surveyed. People want to associate and do business with people they know, like, and trust … with the starting point being trust. Integrity is essential for developing trust, and it remains the single most important building block of enduring success.

INTEGRITY INTERSECTION

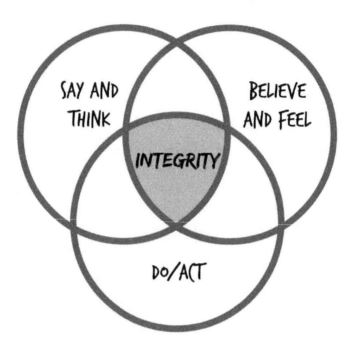

Integrity is found at the intersection of what we say and think, what we believe and feel, and what we do and how we act.

In fact, with so many people prone to serious ethical lapses these days, embracing integrity at every level can actually give your goals or venture a competitive advantage. Is it always easy? Absolutely not … but it's definitely doable!

Here are three important elements to consider when examining how you're showing up around integrity:

★ **Internal Integrity:** Often defined as "doing the right thing even when no one is looking," internal integrity is critical since you must first trust yourself before you can get others to trust you. It can also be the toughest to achieve, since sometimes the person we are least honest with is ourselves!

★ **External Integrity:** This is all about "walking the talk." Do you follow through, meet your commitments, and bring things in on time and budget? One of the biggest killers of external integrity is people who say one thing and do another. Most leaders and businesses can survive a bad economy, but poor external integrity will quickly sink a business (and its leader) in any economy!

★ **Integrated or Whole Integrity:** It's not enough to have either internal or external integrity … they must be combined. Stop for a moment and think about how many famous people you've heard of who lived seemingly exemplary lives with external integrity, but lived a secret personal life devoid of internal integrity and vice versa. Combining the two is where the real magic happens.

Is it always easy, and will you succeed 100% of the time? No one does, but it's important to routinely reflect, recognize when you're out of integrity, and then take ownership and responsibility to make course corrections.

Living and working in integrity often means making painful choices. In those moments, I'm grateful for the enduring words of my high school wrestling coach, "short-term pain brings long-term gain." I'm convinced that growing in the areas of authenticity, transparency, and integrity is like exercising any muscle. It may be painful to push the pile of weights the first time in the gym, but with dedication and small incremental improvement, we can, over time, move the stack with less stress and strain.

In the next section, I share my most important reason to always act ethically. Now more than any other time in history, you have the power to affect countless lives with your actions. It's time to ask yourself the question: what will my legacy be?

The great use of life is to spend it for something that will outlast it.
— William James

Leaving a Legacy of Significance

How would you like people to remember you? It's a question to which you may not have given much thought. After all, we entrepreneurs are doers, not philosophers, right? That said, it *is* important to put some thought into your legacy; into the effect you are having on the world around you and the imprint you will leave behind when you're gone.

Most entrepreneurs think about the tangible assets they'll leave behind when considering their legacies. But in reality, there's far more to your legacy than just money, investments, or property. Your *real* legacy is the impact you had on the people whose lives you touched with your own. You don't simply decide to begin building a legacy right before you die; you *automatically* (and inevitably) begin creating your legacy long before your final days. In the very beginning of this book, I suggested starting out with the end in mind. This is part of what I meant: you should shape your legacy as you build your entrepreneurial career.

> **Your legacy is the impact you had on the people your life touched.**

How many people will you actually touch in your lifetime? Far more than you probably think. Your "Sphere of Influence" includes everyone you contact as you go through life. You have the ability to affect the lives of everyone in your Sphere of Influence, either positively or negatively. That includes your family and friends, of course – but remember, it also includes your vendors, your employees, your customers, and your neighbors.

If you continually pursue excellence with the highest ethical standards in operating your business and your life, you affect your Sphere of Influence positively. But if you start cheating people and your business goes under, many people will be negatively affected. That's an extremely potent motivator: you can positively affect hundreds, if not thousands, of people simply by sticking to your own vision and values.

One of the best ways I know for a person to start considering their legacy is to begin with their own funeral. It may sound a bit morbid, but think about these questions: what do you want people to say about you after you die? What do you want your family to say? How about your team members or your business

---

★ E-INSIGHT ★

Your Sphere of Influence

The world gets smaller every day. We're more interconnected than ever, with more people taking advantage of the possibilities afforded to us by social networking. What does that mean to an entrepreneur? Many things, especially in terms of marketing and staying connected to your clients/customers.

But I want you to think right now in terms of your Sphere of Influence. The fact that we can connect with more people means our reach is longer than it has ever been. You can now touch the lives of people around the world—people you may never meet in person. So, it's time to start asking yourself "how will I use this new interconnectedness to positively impact people's lives? How can I use social media and other tools to really make a difference?"

You might be wondering just how big is your Sphere of Influence? Several years ago, I ran some numbers for myself to find out, and a conservative estimate yielded over 200,000—a number that has undoubtedly grown since then. Even if you own a very small business, your Sphere of Influence could *easily* number in the thousands. Don't sell yourself short … you probably have a much broader reach than you think!

---

competitors? Which charities will show their appreciation because of your contributions?

It's sobering to think in these terms, but I believe it's one of the best ways to help you concentrate on the kind of life you want to live.

Once you visualize what you *want* to happen, it's time to take the next step. Decide what you need to do in order to build the legacy you visualized when you thought about your own funeral. Begin building that life today, ***right now***, so that when the end of your life comes, your legacy will be assured.

★ VICTORY SUCCESS STORY ★

When I got out of the Marines and started my business, I was totally focused on the numbers. I thought it was going to be all about balance sheets, profit and loss statements, and numbers—I thought that's what business was all about. That's what I was taught in business courses in college.

Chris Dambach
Owner – Industry Standard
Co-Owner – empirematerial.com
Owner – Upstate Asbestos
Owner – Bacon Bandits

It is all about the numbers in business, but in life, if your main purpose is strictly business and not family, what kind of life is that? Larry brought that to my attention and taught me, through VICTORY and as my mentor, that you need balance in both areas of business and life. He's been in the #1 instrument in my life for both business and the personal side. And for the first time, I really stopped the music, hopped off the carousel, looked at everything, and weighed and measured everything: my physical health, my financial health, my home life, my relationship with my wife, my relationship with my friends, my spirituality. You're able to measure everything to create a baseline, but what do you do with that? That's what Larry teaches you—how to grow in each area. It's something you don't do once a year, but every day.

At the beginning of last year, I was heading towards a divorce at 100 miles an hour. I was heading towards my kids not knowing who their father was. But business was great at the same time! What does that matter if things aren't good on the home front? Also, my physical health was declining because of stress in the business and my personal life. I was making poor choices, traveling so much for business, and eating on the road.

Larry has shown me how business influences the personal side of things, and it's helped me quite a bit. I've stopped going out with the guys and drinking a few times a week. I've prioritized my relationship with my wife. We have date nights and we go on vacation together. My marriage is much better, much stronger. We have better communication, and we're both learning how important communication is. I now shut my phone off and play with my kids. Sunday is family day—and that makes me feel so much better because it gives me a fire inside come Monday morning.

Another thing Larry taught me is, how do you start your day? Do you start your day complaining about the world, or with positive affirmations? "I'm a good person. I'm an awesome husband, I'm a good father, I'm an amazing business owner to my team members." I say that a few times in the shower and I come out of the shower feeling good, and my smile gets a little wider and I have more pep in my step. It works!

When you're trying to be the best version of you, it influences the people around you without having to say anything or convince them of anything. I have friends and family coming up and saying, "Hey, I notice a difference in you. I'm proud of you." And they're making changes in their lives, too. That's been pretty cool to watch.

Now, it's your turn! Share <u>your</u> *VICTORY* success story with me at success@larrybroughton.me. I'd love to hear from you!

*Everyone has inside of him a piece of good news. The good news is
that you don't know how great you can be! How much you can love!
What you can accomplish! And what your potential is!*
— Anne Frank

★ ACTION STEP: GET TO KNOW YOURSELF ★

Part 1: I talked about this in the last section and now I want you to do it: Take a few minutes to write your own obituary. Assume you lived to a ripe old age and write about the most important aspects of your life as they relate to your business. What was most important to you? To whose lives did you make the greatest contribution? What did your business achieve in your community and in the world at large?

Remember, this obituary should represent what you want to be true at the end of your life. Think about what you want to have achieved, and who you would like to have made an impact on. What will your legacy be to them?

Part 2: Now is the time to reflect deeply on your life, personality, and past. It's critical that you're fair and make an honest assessment of the personal habits which may cause you to fail or succeed.

Take time to list all of the things which seem to be right in your life, in your interpersonal dealings with people, the way you deal with issues, the habits and situations in which you often find yourself, and the specific problems they cause you. Devise a plan to enhance these strengths and positive personality traits. Then identify your weaknesses and character flaws and develop a plan for managing them more effectively.

_____

_____

_____

_____

_____

_____

_____

_____

_____

_____

_____

_____

_____

_____

_____

_____

_____

_____

_____

_____

_____

CHAPTER **8**

DEVELOPING YOUR
VICTORY SUCCESS PLAN

There is no substitute for victory.

Gen. Douglas MacArthur

W e've covered a lot of ground in this book, from Vision to Team and from Intel to Operations. I've asked you to complete the _Kolbe A Index_ and _CliftonStrengths_ assessments to empower yourself, know yourself better, and to become a more effective entrepreneur and leader. I've strongly suggested you reach out to develop a service-based relationship with a mentor and/or hire a coach, and I've challenged you to complete the **Action Step** exercises and break free from the inertia that's keeping you stuck.

So, what have you done so far? Have you taken action on anything? Have you implemented even one idea you've discovered, or have you absorbed the information in this book and filed it away, telling yourself, "I'll get to that tomorrow?"

If you've stepped up and done even one thing, especially something that took you out of your comfort zone, bravo!

If you haven't, then I suggest you pass this book on to someone else – an entrepreneur who will actually *do* something with it. Or you could just throw it into the recycle-bin. Why? Because if you're not already motivated to take action at this point, you're probably not cut out to be an entrepreneur. Ouch! Did that sting a bit?

Now, there's nothing wrong with that, and just the fact that you picked up this book and read it definitely says something about you. You simply may not be ready yet. You may need to hone your skills and confidence working for someone else for a while. That's fine, and I applaud you for recognizing it and making a conscious decision *not* to jump into the entrepreneurial pool with your hands and feet tied. Here's a better idea: put this book on your bookshelf within easy reach and reread the sections that really speak to you as you progress through your career. One day, when you're ready, you'll take action.

Maybe connecting with what it *really* takes to successfully navigate self-employment has created a gnawing fear in your stomach you can't seem to quell. No worries—you likely have some great skills that will make you a valuable team member within someone else's company. In fact, just approaching your job with the entrepreneurial mindset I've laid out in this book will help position you a full head and shoulders above the vast majority of your colleagues. Treating employment as if it were your own business can lead to rapid advancement and significant contributions to your company, your family, and your community.

I've stated it throughout this book: The *key* factor separating highly successful entrepreneurs from those who limp along in mediocrity (or fail completely) is taking rapid, decisive action. If you made it all the way through this book and still did nothing, you failed … badly. So, are you pissed off about that? *Good!*

If you're *serious* about being a high-achieving entrepreneur, clear an hour from your schedule *right now* and use the outline below to immediately start crafting your **VICTORY Success Plan**. But if not—if my challenge still hasn't created even a tiny amount of forward momentum—that's fine. This is where we go our separate ways, and I wish you the very best.

YOUR VICTORY SUCCESS PLAN STARTS NOW! To accomplish this exercise, you will need a notebook/journal/scratch paper, your day-planner or electronic calendar, your favorite pen, and a big red marker. Optional accessories include good thinking music and your favorite adult beverage (or two). Now lock the doors, send the kids to Grandma's, and tell your spouse you need an hour.

Check your watch, write down the time, and get going … you've got one hour, starting *now*!

Whatever the mind can conceive and believe, the mind can achieve.
— Napoleon Hill

Your VICTORY Success Action Plan

<u>VISION</u>

- ★ Take five minutes and write out your company vision statement. Don't self-edit, just let it flow.
- ★ Take five minutes and write out your *personal* vision statement. As above, don't self-edit. Clearly state the income, lifestyle,

accomplishments, and community impact you desire. Commit it to paper.

★ Read each of these back three times with as much energy and gusto as you can muster. Don't be timid—declare out loud what you are all about!

INTEL

★ Take five minutes and write down three specific pieces of information you're missing that are preventing you from making sales, landing the contract you're after, or hiring the right team.

★ Take two minutes and write down one immediate step you can take within the next 24 hours to gain clarity for each of these pieces of Intel. Don't discard ideas as silly or irrelevant—your first gut response is usually the one you should go with!

COACHING

★ Set the timer on your phone or watch for three minutes and make a list of the names of every center of influence you can think of in your industry (or the industry you want to break into). Try for at least ten.

★ Take another two minutes and choose your top three from that list.

★ Set up a "Google Alert" for each name. Over the next two weeks, check the alerts daily and any time one of these three is referenced in an article, interview, or business accomplishment, send a handwritten congratulatory note. In the third note, ask for ten minutes of the recipient's time for a short informational call (you'll be amazed at how many say "yes"). Writing these notes shouldn't take you more than five minutes. Not sure how to set up a Google Alert? Google it!

TEAM BUILDING

★ Dust off your 3-Column Exercise from **Team Building** (Chapter 4), and find the one task or item on the list that really makes your skin crawl or knots up your stomach. Circle it in red. (You'll probably know right away what you want to circle—this should only take about 30 seconds).

★ Make outsourcing, delegating, or deleting this task the top priority on your To-Do list.

★ You'll need 30 minutes to figure out how to make this happen—schedule the 30-minute block on your calendar *right now* and resolve it within the next 12 hours.

★ You now have 48 hours (from the time you make the calendar entry) to *make this a reality*. You'll find that after you knock down the first thing, the others on your list become much easier.

OPERATIONS

★ Imagine you get hit by a truck tomorrow morning on your way to the office. Ouch! The good news: you're alive. The bad news: you won't be doing *anything* for your business over the next week.

★ Take five minutes to identify the top three critical processes or systems that would completely fall apart after your "argument" with the angry truck. Don't BS yourself … write 'em down.

★ Choose the Number One Most Critical System and circle it with your red marker. Reserve a one-hour block on your calendar sometime within the next 24 hours, get on some sort of recording device (iPhones and iPads are great for this), and regurgitate *everything you can think of* about the right way (i.e., your way) to manage this system. Don't skimp on the details: your explanation should be thorough enough that a 15-year old could understand and act on it.

★ Complete this process with all three top systems in the next 48 hours and get all three recordings transcribed. Congrats! You have the beginning of your customized Operations Manual.

RAPID ACTION

★ Take three minutes and write down every single thought or idea you have swirling around in your head right now. If you've actually done everything above, you'll probably be able to list 25 or more easily.

★ Grab your red marker and take one minute to scroll down the list.

★ Circle the first two items that jump off the page at you. Don't think about it, just do it.

★ Schedule 15 minutes of time on your calendar for each item (30 minutes total) within the next 24 hours. Spend that time thinking, doodling, and jotting down everything you can think of about that item.

★ These things popped out at you for a reason, so chances are they're tasks you need to act on immediately. Don't waste time second-guessing yourself—just get into action!

YOU

★ You should be right around the 45-minute mark. I've reserved the most time for you to focus on your most important business asset.

★ Take five minutes total and, on a fresh sheet of paper, write down one specific business goal and one specific personal goal for the next 12 months. Don't be a wuss! You're not looking for run-of-the-mill SMART (Specific, Measurable, Achievable, Realistic, and Timeframe) goals, you're looking for BHAGs (Big Hairy Audacious Goals)!

★ If something immediately pops into your mind and your inner critic starts screaming at you why it can't be done, send them to the woodshed—write it down anyway.

★ Spend five minutes simply connecting with these goals. Think about *who you want to be* to achieve these goals (not necessarily what you need to do). Consider the values and principles you will embody and how accomplishing them will make you feel. Step into how *awesome* accomplishing these goals will be.

★ Take your remaining time (three to five minutes) and complete this declaration:

It's _____ [date one year from today] and it has been the most incredible year! In my business, I've accomplished _____ and in my personal life, I've accomplished _____.
I am proud, excited and thankful.

Now stop, put down your pen, lean back, and take a sip of that favorite beverage…

Congratulations! You just accomplished more strategic planning in a single hour than many entrepreneurs do in an entire year. It wasn't that hard, was it? Religiously and consciously repeat this process every week or two and you'll become an unstoppable entrepreneurial force, regardless of your industry. There are three simple keys to making this work, time and again:

Dedicate one hour per week; mark it on your calendar and make it sacrosanct. Don't overthink things – move fast and don't look back. Write down the first thing that comes to mind and don't second guess yourself.
This process will flush out your inner critics and gremlins. They'll scream, cry, throw things, and make every effort to stick around—to erase the bold and keep on with the old, tired story. Tell them to pound sand! Send them packing.

That's it! It doesn't need to be any more complicated than this. You're now well on your way, and I'm really excited for you. Your **VICTORY Success Plan** is going to make a big impact in your industry, your community, your family, and your life.

And please drop me a line at **succcess@larrybroughton.me** to share your results for this exercise with me … I'd love to hear them, and I promise they'll stay confidential.

CHAPTER 9

FREEDOM ROAD

All our dreams can
come true, if we
have the courage
to pursue them.

Walt Disney

You made it! You are well on your way to VICTORY! In the last few moments that we have together, I want to share my thoughts on the importance of entrepreneurship and the impact your decision to follow the entrepreneur's path has on our nation and the world.

From the depth of my soul, I believe nothing has increased the standard of living more for billions of people, nor lifted more of the world's population out of poverty, than entrepreneurship and capitalism. According to the October 2009 *National Bureau of Economic Research* paper (by Pinkovskiy and Sala-i-Martin) titled, "Parametric Estimations of the World Distribution of Income" (sorry about sounding so wonkish), since 1970, the number of people around the globe living at starvation levels of poverty (on $1 a day or less) has declined by eighty percent.

Interestingly though, most people I speak with believe that worldwide extreme poverty continues to increase due to corporate greed and the mean-spirited business owner. The truth is, however, that increased globalization, expanded property rights, free trade across borders, capitalism, and entrepreneurship have combined to become the biggest anti-poverty initiative, reducing human suffering and misery, the world has ever seen.

Sadly, according to the Harvard IOP Spring 2016 Poll, only 42 percent of young Americans 18 to 29 have a favorable view of capitalism, while 33 percent say they support socialism. Wow! This scares the hell out of me! I've traveled to many communist and socialist countries around the world, and frankly, I prefer capitalism and the positive impact and prosperity it has on every segment of society. Without the innovations and benevolent efforts created by entrepreneurs, billions of global citizens will be left to struggle under the heavy mantel of poverty and squalor.

If capitalism and entrepreneurship has done so much good for the world, why do so many have a negative view about its impact on the economy and society?

Well, the champions, evangelists, and defenders of the virtues of entrepreneurship (us) have mostly remained silent; instead focusing on building our businesses, creating jobs, serving our communities, and slaying the daily dragons of business ownership. We have few vocal advocates who publicly profess the positive impact their ventures are having on their communities … perhaps it's humility, perhaps it's fear of sounding pompous, or perhaps it's fear of ridicule by speaking against the popular assumptions—even though those assumptions are wrong. If you believe, as I do, in the positive power of entrepreneurship and capitalism, please read on.

A leader is one who knows the way, goes the way and shows the way.
— John C. Maxwell

A Crisis of Leadership

Over the past few decades, we've witnessed multiple scandals unfolding in virtually every area of our society: political, financial, religious, and social. We are witnessing the mortgaging of our children's and grandchildren's future by short-sighted politicians who use the labor of the productive to buy the votes of the ever-increasing dependency class. They're spending staggering sums bailing out individuals, companies, and quasi-governmental organizations for bad decisions and poor behavior with zero accountability or regard for the fiscal state of our nation.

Furthermore, we are experiencing an unprecedented leadership vacuum from the halls of Washington, D.C. to state capitols, corporate boardrooms, and beyond. The political elite and the 24/7 news cycle "yammering" class of professional pontificators are far more concerned about *being* right than *doing* right. Cocooned within the detached fantasyland of the D.C. Beltway, they increasingly view the 70 percent of Americans who work hard to raise their children, pay their taxes and mortgages, and want only to create a comfortable life, as little more than serfs.

They compound this view by putting every imaginable barrier in front of those willing to step up and start businesses, from mind-numbingly bizarre regulatory webs to ridiculous employment rules to a confusing labyrinth of confiscatory taxes. Their "mini-me's" in a significant number of state legislatures follow suit, leading to increasingly hostile business environments, especially for start-ups. Finally, they're abetted by a small, but powerful, group of corporate "bad apples" who selfishly seek to protect their own market share, profits, and multimillion dollar bonuses by underwriting ever-increasing barriers to entry for new entrepreneurs.

The net result? Left unchecked, a cycle of crippling job losses, stubbornly high unemployment rates, a growing national security risk as we slide from superpower to debtor-nation, and a generation of Americans leaving their children to inherit a land of reduced opportunities and fewer freedoms. That's where *you* come in—it doesn't have to be this way.

Be the change you wish to see in the world.
— Gandhi

Ready to Take the Lead?

I need *you* to step up and lead. Now, perhaps more than at any other time in our history, America needs its citizens, and its entrepreneurs in particular, to take the lead in our communities, business circles, and even elective offices. It's time for forward thinking men and women of *action*, dedicated to upholding the standards of conduct, values and service that make this country great, to *stand up and be heard*!

We cannot allow the ethical undermining of our country to continue unchallenged. We may not be able to stem the tide in every area, but in our own involvements (especially our businesses, families, and communities), we can show our fellow Americans what honor and integrity *really* look like. I believe entrepreneurs—the *doers* and *innovators*—are perfectly suited to lead the charge to overcome these enormous economic and societal challenges. I implore you: step forward, join me, and *become* the solution … spearhead the Entrepreneur Revolution!

Success is not final, failure is not fatal: it is the
courage to continue that counts.
— Winston Churchill

The Entrepreneur Revolution

I firmly believe entrepreneurship is the clearest path to economic freedom, self-determination, and creating a lasting legacy. Notice I didn't say easiest path! The road can be tough, but you're tougher. I also believe business owners have enormous potential for inciting positive economic and societal change. We have the power to create our own economic stimulus for our families, our communities, our nation, and ourselves.

We can reach out and employ fellow innovators as our businesses grow. We can lead the ethical charge by refusing to compromise our principles or values, and by asking others to do the same. *We can become a driving force* in lifting our country out of this crisis mindset and placing it firmly on the road to freedom once more.

I have dedicated the rest of my professional life to raising and advancing this banner of VICTORY. If you want to succeed in business; if you want to make a positive impact on the world around you; if you want to see your children grow up free, in a world full of opportunities, then step forward, join me, and take up the call. ***Make it happen.***

As this book ends, your journey towards entrepreneurial VICTORY begins. On the next two pages, I leave you with two of my favorite inspirational passages for entrepreneurs that I give to every one of my mastermind members. Some of them have these taped to their desk or pasted into their planner so they can read them daily. I hope they inspire you to take the next steps of your journey with confidence.

The Entrepreneur's Creed

"I do not choose to be a common man.
It is my right to be uncommon … if I can,
I seek opportunity … not security.

I do not wish to be a kept citizen.
Humbled and dulled by having the
State look after me.

I want to take the calculated risk;
To dream and to build.
To fail and to succeed.

I refuse to barter incentive for a dole;
I prefer the challenges of life
To the guaranteed existence;
The thrill of fulfillment
To the stale calm of Utopia.

I will not trade freedom for beneficence
Nor my dignity for a handout;
I will never cower before any master
Nor bend to any threat.

It is my heritage to stand erect.
Proud and unafraid;
To think and act for myself,
To enjoy the benefit of my creations
And to face the world boldly and say:
This, with God's help, I have done
All this is what it means
To be an Entrepreneur."

Author Unknown

The Man in the Arena

"It is not the critic who counts; not the man who points out how the strong man stumbles, or where the doer of deeds could have done them better. The credit belongs to the man who is actually in the arena, whose face is marred by dust and sweat and blood; who strives valiantly; who errs, comes up short again and again, because there is no effort without error and shortcoming; but who does actually strive to do the deeds; who knows the great enthusiasms, the great devotions; who spends himself in a worthy cause; who at the best knows in the end the triumph of high achievement, and who at the worst, if he fails, at least fails while daring greatly, so that his place shall never be with those cold and timid souls who neither know victory nor defeat."

President Theodore Roosevelt
Excerpt from the speech "Citizenship in a Republic"
Given at Sorbonne Paris, France
April 23, 1910

AFTERWORD

By Anthony Melchiorri
Host, Hotel Impossible *on Travel Channel*

If you've gotten this far, it means you've not only read this book, but you're willing to get to the very end. That's a good sign. You've taken the information and insights Larry has offered you, and hopefully worked through all the exercises.

Most of you will close the cover of this book and put it back on a shelf, never to see the light of day again. That's just the life of a book. But this isn't any book. If you've done the work, you now have a VICTORY Success Plan.

Now what do you do?

The harsh reality is, even if you make it past the first year in business, by the fifth year, 50 percent of businesses will close. By year 10? More than 70 percent of businesses will cease operations. To which percentage do you want to belong?

For that small percentage of you who commit to **taking the actions** set forth in this book, you can see growth and change in your business beyond even *your* expectations. I've seen it again and again throughout my 20-year career in the hospitality industry and during my television career with Travel Channel.

If you haven't seen my show *Hotel Impossible*, let me give you a quick sketch of what happens on the show.

A hotel is failing, business isn't good, they're getting negative reviews on travel sites, and the owners or operator call our show to help turn the business around. We look at every process, every guest touch point—basically, everything that makes up a hotel, its business, and the guest experience. We often bring in hospitality experts like Larry, management and financial experts, and we have interior designers redecorate the hotel. Myself and each of these experts give straightforward, no-nonsense advice to the owners, along with hours of consultations and training. Many times (in fact, most of the time) it's hard for the owners to hear.

We leave the hotel owners with a very specific map to get the hotel back on track so the property can stay open, save their image, and attract new clientele. We give it everything we've got, and then … it's up to the hotel owner/operator.

After a few months, we check in with the hotel owner/operator to see what's changed and how they're doing. In almost every case where the owners have taken action to the letter of what we have given them, they can turn around their hotels.

It's the business owners who fail to take action for whatever reason—life happens or they lose enthusiasm or they just get comfortable with failure—and guess what? Their business shows it.

Larry has been on *Hotel Impossible* a number of times and each time he provides the owners and operators many of the same details and insights he's given to you in this book. ***The price you paid for this book is nothing compared to the value of the experience and insight that was poured into it.***

So, let me ask you this: What are you willing to commit? What are you willing to give up to get your business up and running, or back on track? What are you willing to do or stop doing? Are you going to pick and choose from Larry's action items, or go full out?

If you take action, you will see results. It's really just that simple.

Now what do you do?

Whatever you choose to do next, choose to be honest about it. Be honest with yourself. Be honest with your team. Be honest with your family.

People who take ownership of their issues are some of the most courageous people around. It takes courage to admit you don't know everything; it takes courage to admit where you've screwed up; and it takes courage to take the action to move yourself, your business, your team, and your life forward with integrity and excellence. ***Stop reading and start doing!***

To your excellence,

Anthony Melchiorri
HOSPITALITY INDUSTRY EXPERT AND BUSINESS FIXER
Creator and Host of "Hotel Impossible" and "Hotel Impossible: Five Star Secrets," Host of "Hotel Impossible: Showdown"

 @AnthonyHotels

 @AnthonyHotels

LEARN MORE

Thank you for taking the time to read this book. I know from personal experience the lifetime value of just one powerful idea or mindset shift. My goal was to connect you with two or three ideas, resources, or strategies you can immediately implement to improve your business (or initial business plan, if you're just getting started). Honestly, if I've been able to help connect you with just *one* actionable idea or shift, then I've accomplished my mission and would love to hear about it at success@larrybroughton.me.

I believe in you, my fellow entrepreneurs! You are the sole reason I wrote this book. I'm passionate about helping you build the business you desire and create the life you deserve. I want to support you in making a positive impact on your clients/customers, your community, and your family, and living a life of significance. I've been blessed to connect with incredible coaches and mentors as I've grown my own businesses and I'm serious about paying it forward!

I invite you to use the touchpoints below to stay connected. Use them to celebrate your triumphs, learn from your failures, and voice your frustrations or challenges from a place of openness and curiosity so other entrepreneurs facing similar obstacles realize they aren't alone.

Finally, I would like to share my BHAG (Big Hairy Audacious Goal): I want to awaken the enormous latent power for ethical business success within the entrepreneurial community. In short, I'm raising the positive standard of the Entrepreneur Revolution and I invite you to join me.

Staying Connected

Instagram: @larrybroughton
Twitter: @larrybroughton
Facebook: @larrybroughton
Email: info@larrybroughton.me

Online Resources

Listen to the weekly VICTORY podcast online at
www.VictoryPodcast.com and in iTunes.
(Coming soon)

Sign up at **www.yoogozi.com** to find:
  ★ Daily inspiration
  ★ Shareable nuggets of entrepreneur insights
  ★ Cutting edge tools for entrepreneurs
  ★ Success stories from fellow entrepreneurs
  ★ Video, audio, and print interviews with top national entrepreneurs
  ★ Access to mission-tested resources to grow your business and build your team

Kolbe A Index: http://m.kolbe.com/aindex

CliftonStrengths: www.gallupstrengthscenter.com

ABOUT THE AUTHOR

L arry Broughton is an award-winning entrepreneur and CEO, bestselling author, serial entrepreneur, keynote speaker. As a former US Army Staff Sergeant, serving eight years on Special Forces A-Teams (commonly known as the Green Berets), Larry has parlayed the lessons learned from his time in service to his country and applied them to the business arena attaining extraordinary success.

He is the Founder & CEO of broughtonHOTELS, a leader in the boutique hotel industry; and yoogozi.com, an inspirational online learning forum for leaders and high achievers.

Larry has received several business awards, including Ernst & Young's *Entrepreneur of the Year*®; the National Veteran-Owned Business Association's *Vetrepreneur® of the Year*; Coastline Foundation's *Visionary of the Year*; Passkeys Foundation's *National Business*

Leader of Integrity; and Entrepreneur Magazine included his firm on their *Hot 500 List of Fastest Growing Private Companies*.

Larry has authored numerous articles and several books on leadership, team building and entrepreneurial significance, including his newest book, *VICTORY: 7 Revolutionary Strategies for Entrepreneurs to Launch Your Business, Elevate Your Impact and Transform Your Life*, and

FLASHPOINTS for Achievers. His upbeat, creative approach to business and life has been featured in newspaper and magazine articles across the country and he's been a guest on news and TV programs on every major network, including multiple appearances on **CNBC's** *The Big Idea with Donny Deutsch*, **MSNBC's** *Your Business* **with JJ Ramberg, and Travel Channel's hit show,** *Hotel Impossible.*

He has presented to, coached, and mentored thousands of current and aspiring leaders and entrepreneurs across the country. He has delivered keynote addresses and training programs on topics including entrepreneurship, leadership, and overcoming fear and failure to Fortune 100 firms, universities, non-profits, medical facilities, and even the Pentagon's Office of the Chairman of the Joint Chiefs of Staff.

Larry has attended the Executive Program at prestigious Stanford University; studied Russian at the world-renowned Defense Language Institute; and Political Science at University of California, Santa Barbara, and College of San Mateo.

But what he is most proud of is being an involved, available, and intentional father to his two teenage children, Emily and Ben. They teach him about compassion, patience, and how to be the voice of encouragement—and help him be a better boss, mentor, and facilitator.

Larry's personal vision is to help people reach their fullest potential and live lives of true significance. His gift is helping people recognize the talents and gifts they often can't see in themselves, and speaking greatness as often as he can into the business leaders he mentors.

Larry strives to live a life of integrity every day of his life. Sometimes it's exhausting, and it hasn't always been easy, as the ups and downs of his past demonstrate, but those lessons learned along the way are what he brings to each role in which he serves. Whether it's being a dad or a commentator on a TV news program or running his hotel company, he's the same Larry everywhere, all the time.

To learn more about Larry, please visit www.LarryBroughton.me, www.yoogozi.com, and www.broughtonHOTELS.com.

THE IDEAL SPEAKER FOR YOUR NEXT EVENT

Larry is one of the country's most popular leadership speakers who provides high-octane, informative, and inspirational keynote presentations for corporations, non-profits, governmental agencies, military organizations, conferences, seminars, award ceremonies, colleges and universities, associations, entrepreneur groups, and fundraising events.

Find out why dozens of organizations around the world call Larry the most inspiring, authentic, and motivating speaker they've ever had! Matt Brauning, the Founder of Evolution Seminars, said, *"Larry ... absolutely blew the roof off! I have never heard so much positive feedback from ANY speaker, and we've put on nearly 200 seminars. Larry is authentic, powerful in his message, and inspiring to the heart."*

Larry's unique and moving stories of triumph and tragedy, business success, leadership principles, and his path towards significance leaves audiences with practical tips and teaching points and energized to take action.

To see Larry's speaker reel, or to invite him to speak at an event, please visit: <u>www.LarryBroughton.me/speaker</u>.

CPSIA information can be obtained
at www.ICGtesting.com
Printed in the USA
FSHW022359250321
79868FS